Dear Douglas —
Blessings on you
& your ministry!
Warmly,
Michelle

Incorporating Children in Worship

Incorporating
Children in Worship

MARK OF THE KINGDOM

Michelle A. Clifton-Soderstrom
and David D. Bjorlin

Foreword by
William H. Willimon

CASCADE *Books* • Eugene, Oregon

INCORPORATING CHILDREN IN WORSHIP
Mark of the Kingdom

Cascade Books
An Imprint of Wipf and Stock Publishers
199 W. 8th Ave., Suite 3
Eugene, OR 97401

www.wipfandstock.com

ISBN 13: 978-1-62032-621-3

Cataloging-in-Publication data:

Clifton-Soderstrom, Michelle A., and Bjorlin, David D.

Incorporating children in worship : mark of the kingdom / Michelle A. Clifton-Soderstrom and David D. Bjorlin; foreword by William H. Willimon.

xiv + 152 p.; 23 cm—Includes bibliographical references.

ISBN 13: 978-1-62032-621-3

1. Children in public worship. 2. Worship (Religious education). 3. Children—Biblical teaching. I. Title.

BV26.2 C38 2014

Manufactured in the USA.

To those children who formed us in worship

And to Richard whose child-like faith incorporated all…

The kingdom of God is like a mustard seed that, when it is sown in the ground, is smaller than all of the seeds on earth.

MARK 4:31

Contents

Foreword by William H. Willimon ix

Acknowledgments xi

Introduction 1

1 Children 11

2 Worship 31

3 Incorporation 53

4 Virtue 76

5 Vocation 101

6 Vision 125

Conclusion 139

Bibliography 145

Foreword

Jesus was teaching with everyone gathered around, all attempting to pay attention (Luke 18). In the middle of Jesus' theological commentary one of the grownups in the class shouted in exasperation, "Send these kids away! Don't we have children's church or a nursery or something to get rid of them?" A couple of children were scuffling in the dust.

"I'm being distracted by these unruly kids," one of the adults complained.

And do you remember what Jesus did on that occasion? He took a child in his arms, embracing the one whom the crowd wanted to send away. Then in an evocative act Jesus placed the child "in the midst of them," as if to say, "I am placing the child at the center in order to help you pay attention. The kingdom of God belongs to such as these."

I'm sure that some of the most revolutionary, countercultural statements that Jesus made were his comments about children. In our kingdoms, children are a burden, a distraction, or competitors for adult attentiveness. But in the realm of God, helpless, dependent, vulnerable, marginalized children are at the center, the point of Incarnation.

In this wonderful book, Michelle A. Clifton-Soderstrom and David D. Bjorlin speak up for "the deep integration of children that reflects the triune God and the gifts that children have to offer." In so doing they lead us to greater fidelity to the Savior who comes to us as a child and thereby demands to be received as a child. We are thus reminded that children are at the center of the church's life not simply because we need children in order for our church to have a future but rather because Jesus put children at the center. We can't be faithful to Christ without relating to children as Jesus relates to children. As Jesus said, we can't even hope to enter God's realm except as little children.

My denominational family has a problem (I expect yours does too) in that we are aging away. We have not been faithful in attracting children or in retention of our young. This book on welcoming children and integrating them fully into the life of the church was written for a time such as this. I saw a study a few years ago that proved to me that those churches that remove their children from worship on Sunday (banishing them to "children's church") have a difficult time of retaining their children in their church as the children grow up. Those churches that lovingly find a way to keep their children with them on Sunday tend to keep their children throughout their lives. We must not squander the most formative years of our children's lives by removing them from the central, defining act of the Christian faith—the Sunday worship of the congregation. Nor must we waste the invitation to new life and vitality that God gives us in giving us children.

I therefore pray that this book will be used by God to stir our churches to full commitment to the full inclusion of children in Sunday worship and in every area of church life. I also hope that this book will induce us to purge ourselves of any practices that imply that God's children are not full and valued members of our fellowship. Our Lord has expressly given little children a place at the center of his kingdom. We are not in any way to hinder or to forbid them. Let's pray that the message as well as the practical ideas in this book will be used by God to give us the determination and the creativity truly to include our young in our church.

William H. Willimon
Professor of the Practice of Christian Ministry, Duke Divinity School

Acknowledgments

All books are a culmination of sorts. They are a culmination of ideas, influences, and people that have coalesced around a theme or idea that one has been compelled to write about. This book is no different. Thus, acknowledgements are a way to point to the many streams that have fed the creation of this book, without which such an undertaking would be impossible.

We thank Rachel Jurkowski, who tracked down sources, compiled the bibliography, edited the first rough draft, and did the other often over-looked tasks that are essential to a book's completion with skill and joy. We also are grateful to Cathy Norman Peterson, whose expert editing of the manuscript strengthened it both technically and conceptually. We thank Will Willimon not only for the foreword but for his passion for ministry and for creatively preaching the gospel. We would also like to thank the North Park Theological Seminary community, where we have been formed as students, academics, and disciples of Christ. Finally, we are grateful to Rodney Clapp and the entire team at Wipf and Stock, whose support made this book a reality.

Each of us also acknowledges the people that have encouraged us individually. For me (Dave), the majority of my adult knowledge of children came during five summers at Hermantown KidCare, a kindergarten-fifth grade summer day camp in Northern Minnesota where I worked during my college years. Thank you to the children, parents, and staff who gave me that gift. Further, I acknowledge the teachers, professors, and pastors that have formed me into the writer, theologian, liturgist, and person I am. I especially thank Jerry Kaldor, Jan Peterson, Jeanne Shermer, Beth Clark, Keith Swanson, Dawn Griffith, Neil Witikko, Baxter and Margie Swenson, Tammy Swanson-Draheim, Aaron Johnson, Kurt Peterson, Theodora Ayot, Phil Anderson, Phillis Sheppard, Brent Laytham, Karen Westerfield Tucker, and Richard Carlson. In the compassionate and skilled hands of these teachers and pastors my life has been formed. Thank you to my own family who cared for and loved the child in their midst: Dean, Marijo, Jessica, Isaac, Stephen, Anna, and Peter. Further, I am grateful for my two nieces, Daphne and Paisley, who have again reminded me of the joy and wonder of childhood. Finally, I would be remiss if I did not thank Michelle. Not only did she graciously invite a greenhorn like me into this project, she has also been my skilled teacher, compassionate mentor, and dear friend. Her life as a parent and spouse, a professor and mentor to future pastors, a writer and academic for the church, and a friend to many serves as a model that I continually seek to emulate.

I (Michelle) echo Dave's appreciation of children in the formulation of this book. When my daughter Hannah filled out the attendance book in the church pew, adding the names of Charles Wesley and Lina Sandell because we had sung their hymns that morning, I knew this book needed to be written. Children have much to teach us in worship, and the idea of the cloud of witnesses evoked by an eight-year-old is just one of the many ways I've been formed in worship by my children, Hannah and Johannes. They ask what the colors mean or why we aren't having communion every week, and they also remind me that we receive (rather than take) grace and that God is more than a God who fulfills our individual needs. For them, I give thanks, along with all of the children and youth who witness to the good news of Christ in worship.

For my dear friend Cathy, who not only offered editing but more importantly support and encouragement in every season, I am grateful. She adds much to my life and my work. I am also wonderfully indebted to those pastors and educators who work creatively to incorporate children in worship—Steve Burger, Linda Cannell, Paula Frost, Katie Isaza, and my children's pastors Elise Brimhall and Libby Piotrowski. They are truly humble before children and their work is inspiring. I am also tremendously blessed by Dave's work in this manuscript. With one foot in the pastorate and the other in the academy, his knowledge, expertise, creativity, and discipline have made this book a contribution to the whole church. Finally, I offer my deep gratitude to my husband Karl for believing that I have something to offer Christ's church and for supporting my work wholeheartedly. He remains one of God's greatest gifts to me.

We conclude our acknowledgements with the deepest appreciation for the central role children have played in both of our lives. Children challenge, instruct, prod, and inspire us to think differently about our faith and our world. It is primarily their voice that we have heard and responded to in the pages that follow.

David D. Bjorlin
Michelle A. Clifton-Soderstrom
Advent, 2013

Introduction

The Church of All Creatures Great and Small wants to live up to its name. Worship begins with a prelude, call to worship, and invocation. The congregation sings the hymn of adoration and praise. The liturgist then leads with a prayer of confession, the pastor offers words of assurance, and the people pass the peace. After they read Scripture, the pastor comes down from the pulpit and extends an invitation: "Would all of the adults please come to the front for a 'Moment for the Grown-Ups'?"

The children and youth watch the adults file up in orderly fashion and sit on the floor around the pastor—except one who makes a beeline for the restroom. The grown-up sermon is an object lesson, using John 6 to describe Jesus as the bread of life. Moving from people's need for good food to their dependence on the good Lord, the pastor inquires, "Can anyone tell me what your favorite food is?" One man who is diabetic shouts out, "Candy!" All of the children in the pews giggle. Another woman who works as a chef offers, "Boeuf bourguignon!" Sitting a few rows back, her daughter sits up and smiles proudly. Suddenly, the man who was on a bathroom break returns. He apparently has heard the question over the sound system, and wants to participate. "I really enjoy Bud Light!" he jokes. As the children and youth erupt with laughter, the joker's own teenaged son slinks down in his seat, embarrassed by his father's gaffe.

The pastor forges ahead, finishing the message, and then dismisses the adults downstairs to do crafts and have a snack. Once they have left, he gets down to the business of worship—launching into a sermon about Jesus as the bread of life. He preaches about the remarkable young boy who shares his loaves and fish. He amplifies that way Jesus uses the boy to feed the adults and nourish the crowd of people. The pastor emphasizes that even though the boy is young, unprepared, and a little unclear about what Jesus is doing, he nevertheless has much to offer—food for 5,000! The pastor's

1

sermon culminates with the connection between Jesus and the bread that is the nourishment sustaining those who follow him. The inspired children see themselves in God's story. They draw pictures of the boy talking with Jesus, sneak peeks at the communion bread on the table, and dance around the pews reflecting the chaotic scene that Jesus himself faced. Many of the children wonder how in the world Jesus could turn into bread.

As the sermon concludes, the few children who are still seated stand to sing. The adults silently rejoin the children and youth in the pews, taking their places with little notice. Communion follows, and the congregation is invited forward for the sacred meal. The children respond to the sermon by making the pilgrimage down the aisle to the table. Some whisper, "Did the little boy bring this loaf?" Another asks where the fish is. One remarks, "I'm so thirsty!" and heads toward the juice first. Still others tell the servers how much the warm bread reminds them of home. One young child even says, "Jesus tastes *really* good today!" The pastor marvels at the children's faith as it leads him to a new vantage point from which to view the story of God.

Many adults, on the other hand, remain seated. Some are not prepared. Others are hesitant because they are unclear about what is *really* going on. Still more feel unworthy to participate. The pastor is taken by surprise at the adults' response in contrast to the children's. Looking up to the cross, he questions the congregation's long tradition of dismissing the adults for part of the worship and wonders whether he might change that culture in the future. He sadly realizes that perhaps even grown-ups need more than a "moment."

The scenario above mirrors the assumptions entrenched within the church regarding the place of adults—and children—in worship. You may be tempted to dismiss the scenario with little reflection, writing it off as unfeasible. Or perhaps the illustration moves you to reflect on how worship might progress if children and youth were central to the identity of the congregation. Even better, you may envision what worship might look like were the whole congregation—including adults, pastors, and worship planners—to incorporate children fully into worship.

Many congregations are indeed attentive to the children in their midst and plan their services with them in mind. While attention to children and their participation is important, in this book we are pursuing the deep integration of children that reflects the triune God and the gifts that children have to offer. Evangelical Covenant pastor of intergenerational ministries Steve Burger offers a template for analyzing the place of children in worship as it reflects how congregations integrate children to greater or lesser degrees. The template includes three questions: 1) Are children participating? 2) Are children engaged? and 3) Do children have voice?[1] Burger's questions are useful for congregations that want to move from participation in certain aspects of the service to full incorporation in the whole movement of worship. For example, a child playing a tambourine along with the worship band is an excellent starting point. A child playing a tambourine and drawing a picture that reflects the Lord's Prayer after it is prayed is yet another level of integration. A child playing a tambourine, drawing a picture, and proclaiming at the table, "I'm so thirsty!" heralds the good news that Christ is coming—if people are listening. The remark indicating the child's bodily needs could be received as a disrespectful interruption in the communion line. Conversely, the exclamation "I'm so thirsty" could be interpreted in the context of John's words late in Revelation: "Come. And let everyone who is thirsty come" (Rev 22:17). The child is thirsty, and the congregation who accepts the child's expectant voice becomes more deeply drawn into the corporate flow of worship, even allowing the story to continue by remembering Jesus' reply to the thirsty: "Surely I am coming soon" (Rev 22:20).

What Is *Incorporating Children in Worship* About?

We contend that incorporating children in the mission of the church is a mark of the kingdom of God and as such calls for a set of practices that are distinctive to the church's identity. Because worship is the primary ritual through which the church glorifies God and through which God sanctifies humanity, we maintain that worship is the decisive occasion for the church to incorporate children. We contend that incorporating children is a powerful and overlooked mark of God's kingdom that signifies not only a vibrant, faithful communion but also offers a critical window into the Spirit's work of linking the church to Christ.

We use the language of "mark" and "kingdom" with intention. Traditionally marks have been articulated as the signs, descriptors, or characteristics of the people of God. According to Luther, marks are "holy possessions whereby the Holy Spirit effects in us a daily sanctification and vivification in Christ."[2] Marks indicate the characteristics that are central to the church's

1. Burger, "Christian Formation."
2. Luther, "On the Councils of the Church," 166.

identity and mission. Additionally, marks of the church find their source in the divine life, and in particular in the call of Christ to realize the faithful's role in the kingdom. Finally, the church's marks point to the activity of the triune God in the world. In these ways, we refer to "marks" in our argument for the full incorporation of children. God is doing something in the life of the body when children are participants in worship, and in this ecclesial ritual, the body of Christ heralds the unity of the people of God.

The use of "kingdom" in both Scripture and the Christian tradition is rich and complex, so we highlight only some of the features apposite to this book. As a preacher, Jesus announced the kingdom of God in most of his sermons. The Gospel accounts attest to this truth. "The time is fulfilled, and the kingdom of God has come near," readers hear from Mark and Matthew (Mark 1:15; see also Matt 4:17). Jesus makes clear that the kingdom is about God's reign and that the advancing kingdom is good and liberating news.

Most biblical scholars view the kingdom as both a present and future reality, in that God's kingdom has made itself known in Jesus and will come to completion at the eschaton. It includes earthly and heavenly dimensions as they point to the fullness of God's creative purposes. The kingdom of God/heaven refers to God's reign connected with redemption in Jesus Christ and the final consummation of creation. It is, therefore, God's dynamic action in which humans participate even though they are not the effective source or even primary agent.

Jesus' kingdom preaching acknowledged God's creative purposes and offered an ethic of welcoming God's reign. In Jesus, one sees both the authority of God as well as the confirmation of God's reign through Jesus' mighty works. Jesus attributes his work for the kingdom to the Father; yet Jesus and the Father are one. In their unitive work, God announces humanity's own role in receiving God's power and grace and responding cooperatively. Hence, a mark of the people of God engaged in God's mission is that of shaping the world according to Jesus' vision of the kingdom. Humanity is given both the vision and power to shape the world for the purposes of advancing the kingdom.

The descriptions in Matthew's and Mark's Gospels of entering the kingdom as a child are particularly salient. We examine the meaning of Jesus' words in greater depth in chapter 1, but it is important here to note the child's faith is a presupposition for entering into the kingdom of heaven (Matt 18:3; Mark 10:4). Reformed theologian David Jensen argues that Jesus' proclamation of the kingdom of God is inseparable from his care for the vulnerable and most especially children.[3] Liberation theologian Jon Sobrino elaborates on the connection between the kingdom and the vulnerable, contending that the good news about the kingdom of God has recipients, or addressees. Luke's Gospel reveals the addressees generally as the poor. Sobrino fleshes out the meaning of "poor" as the economic poor and the sociological poor—those who are the little ones, the least of these, and whose full dignity is denied.[4] Children fit this category, and Jesus embodies the connection in his preferential care for children. Care that reflects Jesus' own preference for the poor is central to the work of the kingdom. Neglect of the poor and least of these is contrary to the kindgom, and Sobrino calls such neglect the "anti-kingdom."[5] As a manifestation of the least of these and little ones, children embody the very heart of Jesus' message in which care for the poor is a distinctive mark of the advancement of God's kingdom.

The particular activity that forms Christians for the work of the kingdom, or God's mission, is worship. Worship constitutes the single most important activity in which the church engages and, further, it is the time when the body comes together regularly, forming its identity as coworkers with Christ in advancing God's kingdom. The full inclusion of children in worship is one of the ways that the church announces God's reign in a distinctive way. If Sobrino is right about the anti-kingdom constituting that which detracts from Jesus' proclamation of the kingdom and care for the poor and least of these, then that which we proclaim and practice in worship connects deeply with God's reign. In other words, the inclusion of children in the distinctive activities of the church matters to the advancement of God's kingdom on earth.

Why Read about Children and Worship?

Many scholarly works deal with the themes of children and worship. Few, however, deal with the critical intersection of children and worship in a theological and ecumenical way. The scholarly task of articulating children's place in the worshiping life is worthy of interacting with the rich resources in the church's tradition. We utilize works of contemporary and historical theologians, including early Christian sources. We also intentionally

3. Jensen, *Graced Vulnerability*, 22–23.
4. Sobrino, *Jesus the Liberator*, 80.
5. Ibid., 72.

engage texts from scholars of color and women who have critical insights into vulnerability and marginalization generally, as well as children par-' ticularly. We take an interdisciplinary approach, focusing on the fields of theology, liturgy, Scripture, and ethics.

Current literature dealing with children offers much to our work. Biblical scholars such as Judith Gundry, Beverly Gaventa, Reidar Aasgaard, and Jacqueline Lapsley develop the place and role of children in Scripture in significant ways. Theologians and Christian ethicists have written many books that contribute to work in the area of children as well. Among these, Joyce Ann Mercer, Bonnie Miller-McLemore, Amy Laura Hall, and Martin Marty stand out in their ability to shift traditional paradigms pertaining to children. Marcia Bunge's two edited volumes, *The Child in Christian Thought* and *The Child in the Bible*, have also done groundbreaking work on children in the history of the church. For an idea of the place of children in the Greco-Roman period and the early history of the church, the historical work of O. M. Bakke, Cornelia Horn, and John Martens is notable.

Our use of "child" and "children" is intentionally broad. The point is not to delineate the faith development of children specifically. The corpus of Catholic nun and Hebrew scholar Sofia Cavalletti attends to children's faith development in the context of religious education and liturgy.[6] Her approach informs this book as she attends to the wonder of the child and the child's place in liturgy. Our task as it relates to children is to theologically ground the incorporation of children as "other" into the body, and while we use the category of children, our work applies to youth as well.

Other theologians and philosophers who help frame the contours of this book include Samuel Wells, whose work on drama, improvisation, and Christian ethics shapes our thinking. Willie James Jennings's and Brian Bantum's work on race and ethnicity supplement our approach to children as other. In chapters 4 and 5, we rely on Alasdair MacIntyre's *After Virtue* to analyze worship as a social practice. Karl Clifton-Soderstrom's phenomenological analyses of the virtues facilitates our development of virtue particularly as we applied it to the character of children.

Along with such thinkers as William Willimon, Stephen Wilson, James K. A. Smith, Don Saliers, and others, we argue that liturgy can and ought to be linked with other ecclesial practices, such as hospitality, charity,

---

6. For work by Cavalletti, see titles in the bibliography. Cavalletti brilliantly combines the fields of liturgy, Scripture, religious education, and faith development in the context of children.

and inclusion. Indeed, worship and liturgy shape the church's life outside of worship and constitute the place where the believing community receives and lives out its identity. Christian formation thinkers who offer exceptional paradigms and practical ideas for working with children in worship include Sofia Cavelletti, Jerome Berryman, Scottie Mae, and Linda Cannell.

In this work, we attend to that intersection in a manner that engages not only contemporary work but also the historical treasures in the Christian tradition. Practical theologian and retired United Methodist bishop William Willimon argues, "Some of the most radical liturgical innovation has occurred in the most 'ritualized' churches. Only the person who is secure in his or her identity can afford the risk and the threat that come from experimentation with new forms of being and acting."[7] Wholeheartedly agreeing with Willimon, we believe that a theological foundation that connects with Scripture and the church's history aids the creative work of worship and liturgy. This book offers such a foundation as it pertains to the work of incorporating children in worship.

Who Should Read about Children and Worship?

We write for a broad audience. Pastors, students, parents, Christian educators, and anyone who desires to facilitate greater participation on the part of the children and youth comprise our target audience. While some of the analyses are geared toward pastors and theologically educated readers, the themes of the book are accessible to any who work with children, including parents. We offer examples throughout that crystallize our arguments—especially in cases of the more complex arguments, such as those in chapters 3 and 4. These examples are meant to clarify and spark further thought on creative and practical ways to incorporate children.

Our own ecclesial tradition is the Evangelical Covenant Church; yet our interlocutors include scholars and pastors from other evangelical traditions, as well as the United Methodist, Lutheran, Reformed, Roman Catholic, and Episcopal traditions. The ways we develop the themes of social practices, moral formation, and identity are fitting to any Christian tradition. They are also translatable to other religious traditions, such as Judaism, which desires to incorporate children in sacred rituals.

The first part of the book engages the themes of children, worship, and incorporation through biblical and theological lenses. We examine who

7. Willimon, *The Service of God*, 47.

children are in God's redemptive story, how worship engages the drama of salvation, and what God's life in Trinity and the two natures of Christ offer in terms of incorporating difference in unity. These chapters offer a foundation for the second half of the book, where we offer a comprehensive look at the ways children gift the worshiping body through the themes of virtue and vocation. We end with a vision for God's church that challenges Christians to think and act in ways that humbly open the doors to all kinds of difference. The ability of the community of faith to demonstrate humility before children reveals possibilities for the faithful to incorporate other, perhaps more threatening, kinds of difference. Children offer an avenue into the unified yet diverse reality of all God's creatures.

This book is intended to complement courses that have practical outcomes but also desire to work with historical and theological themes. Our footnotes and bibliography are extensive, and professors and scholars interested in the intersection of children and worship will find much to engage. Courses on children's ministry, youth ministry, Christian formation, worship, and moral theology will find useful material to discuss and analyze. We suggest working through the book in two parts, using the first (chapters 1–3) to dialogue with the biblical, historical, and theological tradition and the second (chapters 4–6) to think creatively about the formation of virtue in the practice of worship.

We encourage parents and pastors who read this book to do so in groups, whether in adult Sunday school or small groups. The themes herein are meant to inspire pastors and parents to think differently about children in worship, as well as to develop creative practices that work for particular congregations and the ways they worship. This might encourage parents to intentionally prepare their child for worship throughout the week, perhaps by memorizing the Lord's Prayer or the refrain of a song or hymn. It also might inspire parents to include seasonal symbols, such as an Advent wreath, or seasonal practices, such as Lenten disciplines, in family life outside of worship. We believe that congregations whose members and participants support one another have greater potential for growth and transformation.

With formation in mind, we invite you to read this book with an open heart for children who are both "other" and united in Christ's body. God's grace often works in that which is small, and God's saving history would look radically different without children—to the point that it would not be recognizable as Christianity. God gifts Israel with children. God gifts the church with children. We teach them, and they teach us—they even *save* us. Without them, we risk the possibility of becoming rigid and overly bound. With them, we risk the possibility of being challenged and transformed. Perhaps we even give them more than a moment and find the kingdom of heaven anew.

Children
Worship
Incorporation
Virtue
Vocation
Vision

1. Children

If you tour Joe's parish in Chicago, he will tell you that the front doors of a church are called portals. Joe is a church artist and points out that doors take persons from one bounded place to the next. Portals do more—they allow participants to pass from the quotidian into the sacred space of the people of God. Will Willimon writes, "In past times, when the Christian entered the sanctuary and its liturgy, it was not a matter of leaving the world, but rather of entering the world as it *really* looked in its full, transparent reality—as the place of God's love and activity."[1] Portals open into the sanctuary, where the faithful enact the Christian story, form their faith through worship, and offer themselves to the kingdom of heaven.

Young Brooke grasps the idea of portals instinctively. When I (Michelle) entered the doors of her church for the first time, she exclaimed, "Michelle, that's my church! It doesn't look that big on the outside, but inside, it's really big!" Brooke's church refers to the people she knows, the stories she indwells, and the sacred spaces she freely navigates. "Really big" reveals the truth about what lies within the church portals, where Brooke is an active participant in a believing community that lets God in. Brooke is not leaving the real world when she goes to church—she is entering the world as it *really* is. God's kingdom reigns within the seemingly small

1. Willimon, *Service of God*, 52.

exterior of Bethany Covenant Church, and it is doing big things for young Brooke.

Brooke's discerning ecclesiology of perceiving the big in the small applies to many other aspects of the kingdom of God. Throughout Scripture, God works through people or images that seem small in order to communicate big truths. The woman of 1 Kings 17 possesses only a handful of meal and a tiny bit of oil, yet these sustain the great prophet Elijah. The poor widow in Mark who casts two mites into the treasury gives the most, Jesus says, because she gives all she has. Five loaves and two fish equal food for more than five thousand? God fills the biblical narratives repeatedly by creating something from nothing. Readers learn to expect that in God's economy, every little bit—and most especially every little bit—counts.

Children constitute a significant path through which God works in the small to advance the bigness of the kingdom. "Welcome the little children," Scripture urges. "The one who welcomes the least of these welcomes me and my Father," Jesus says in the Gospel narratives. Jesus' behavior toward children is striking, and the meaning of his actions communicates an often overlooked truth: children are integral members of Christ's church. They have something big to offer the advancement of God's kingdom on earth.

Additionally, children embody God's kingdom in unique ways. In his book on improvisation and Christian ethics, Samuel Wells notes that the most faithful responses are often the most obvious.[2] Children tend to be obvious, and when adults take more than a moment to pay attention to their messages—both verbal and nonverbal—they open themselves to some of the obvious ways that God is working in their midst. Philosopher and educator James K. A. Smith begins his book *Desiring the Kingdom* with these words: "For Madison: That little glint in your eye is, for me, a sure sign that the kingdom is a kingdom of love."[3] Smith's dedication is noteworthy, for he attributes to a child the evidence that love constitutes God's kingdom. Although his book takes on the complex themes of liturgy, desire, and Christian formation in order to envision God's kingdom, young Madison's glint—something so small that Smith must have paid attention in order to catch it—reveals with clarity the obvious truth that the kingdom is a kingdom of love. Every little bit counts in God's kingdom, and that is the interest and pursuit of our work overall and this chapter in particular.

2. Wells, *Improvisation*, 67.

3. Smith, *Desiring the Kingdom*.

In the introduction, we affirmed that incorporating children is a mark of the kingdom. Incorporating children signifies a vibrant, faithful communion, and it also offers a critical window into the Spirit's work of linking the church to Christ. This chapter addresses the above two aspects of our thesis. First, we explore why children's incorporation signifies faithful worship by looking at the child in the biblical narrative and how children are important to the communities God calls. Second, we show how children's incorporation provides insight into the Spirit's work of linking the church to Christ. In this section, we focus on the child as a trope in Scripture. Biblical writers use the child as a trope in multifaceted ways to reveal the contours of faithful relationship with God. In marking humanity's path with God, the trope of the (small) child expands the (big) vision of the Spirit, conjoining members of the body with one another and with Christ. These sections culminate with the good news about the small: our very big God became a small child. Throughout the trajectory of Scripture, not only are children lifted up as both people and as trope, but most importantly, God enters human history in the form of a Child. The final section celebrates the big news of the Christ-child.

Children: Blessed Participants

Valued in Themselves

Presbyterian churches typically call on *all* members of the congregation to become godparents to the child being baptized. The congregation's vows include promises to undertake responsibility for children who are not their own, biologically speaking, and to practice this responsibility for the glory of God. While this is a tall order for all members to assume, it is close to Jesus' promise to his disciples: "I will not leave you orphaned; I am coming to you" (John 14:18).

The kingdom of God has ample room for the small, and God's heart for the child is perhaps best revealed in Scripture's attention to the orphan. Psalm 10:14 describes Yahweh as the helper of orphans, a sign that God also helps all who are helpless. The biblical narrative recognizes children's vulnerability and calls the Israelite people to respond by ensuring their care. In fact, Israel's faithfulness is measured by how it cares for the orphan, among others. This test is also found in James 1:27 as a measure of genuine religion.

In addition to care, Isaiah exhorts Israel to execute justice for the orphan (Isa 1:17). Neglect in these areas of care and justice evokes God's judgment. God recognizes the plight of orphans, works to overcome it, and ensures that none—even the smallest among them—will be left alone. The injunction to care for the orphan in the entirety of both Testaments solidifies the value of the most oppressed children. The depth of God's love, care, and justice endows children who are not even part of a familial heritage with inherent worth.

Children also have a central place in God's blessing. The command for humans to be fruitful and multiply occurs in the context of God blessing humankind. Israel's blessing passes through children, and they are valued recipients of God's call to be a people. The sign of blessing is circumcision, the mark of which denotes that children are initiated into the covenant, heirs of God's promise, and part of God's creation of a new people.

Fertility is a blessing and a *mitzvot*, or command, in Jewish theology. Readers of Scripture know that children are deeply valued because of the suffering involved in barrenness. Barrenness is portrayed as one of the greatest sufferings a human being can experience (e.g., the Genesis matriarchal narratives, Proverbs 30:15–16).[4] Children are evidence of God's blessing, not only in a biological or reproductive framework, but also as gifts for the entire human community. Children belong to God, as Hannah recognizes in her willingness to give Samuel over to God's service. All God's people are integrally connected by sharing in the care and the fate of children. Often the larger community ensures children's survival and flourishing. Pharaoh's daughter exemplifies (somewhat ironically) the potential of non-family members in the care of children when she takes in baby Moses. The people of God, in other words, are charged to steward their blessings together and in broad-minded ways.

Children also represent the vastness of God's promises and faithfulness. According to Judith Gundry-Volf, children have great significance and important roles in Old Testament-Jewish tradition.[5] Children are made in the image of God, and this image is a gift that grows over time. Biblical scholar W. Sibley Towner applies the image of God to all human beings universally and describes its growth. "The *imago dei* is displayed in individuals and communities differently as maturation, experience, or

---

4. For more on this, see Michelle Clifton-Soderstrom, "Beyond the Blessed/Cursed Dichotomy."

5. Gundry-Volf, "The Least and the Greatest," 34.

character-building take place."[6] The process of maturation assumes the existence of the *imago dei* and inherently affirms that the young bear God's image in their very potential to grow and mature in faith.

The New Testament similarly testifies to the value of children. The Gospel of Mark shows a particularly high regard for the status of children. In her book *Welcoming Children*, Joyce Ann Mercer discusses the themes of God's reign and the centrality of social status as it pertains to children in Mark's Gospel. The contrasts between the empire of Rome and the kingdom of God form the foreground for understanding the place of children and the significance of Jesus' responses to them. Mercer notes descriptive themes of the kingdom of God in Mark. Mark portrays communities who follow the way of Jesus as communities where the most vulnerable thrive, the least powerful are valued, and disciples live in radical solidarity with one another. Moreover, these discipleship communities engage unjust and corrupt power structures as part of new life in Christ.[7]

Mercer also refers to Mark's Gospel as a counter-narrative to power structures that foster particular hardships for children and other marginalized groups.[8] Specifically, Mark uses children to move the story along, and through this lens, Mercer constructs what she calls a liberatory theology of childhood, defined by God's purposes for children. She writes, "God gives children to the church and the world so that God may be known."[9] In other words, the value of blessing is not only for children; God's blessing liberates children for participation in God's kingdom and is liberating for all through their witness.

Valued as Participants

A book about the young Queen Esther has inhabited my (Michelle's) daughter's bookshelf since she was three. Even before my daughter, who is now thirteen, could read, Esther's story came to life in the form of pictures, and she paged through the book more times than I can recall. It is easy to understand why: my daughter identified with the small, and she recognized the big. Small Esther had a big mission, and she fulfilled it courageously. Esther protected her people before a powerful king who had his first wife

6. Towner, "Children and the Image of God," 320–21.

7. Mercer, *Welcoming Children*, 45–46.

8. Ibid., 44–45.

9. Ibid., 66.

killed and who ruled a country that had imprisoned the Jews and subverted Jewish culture. Though Esther was young, she knew who she was (Jewish), and she had her cousin Mordecai's support. The title of the book is *Queen Esther Saves Her People*, and while one might rightly take issue with exactly who is doing the work of saving, it is nevertheless remarkable that such a young girl played a significant role in God's saving work.[10]

Children are important actors in the unfolding drama of the kingdom of God, and the desire to read stories such as Esther's at a young age reveals a yearning in children to participate in stories that are bigger than them (a concept we develop further in the following chapter). Children in Scripture play vital roles in covenant identity and worship. In the narratives of Esther and David, for example, God ordains youth to dangerous positions, and they respond faithfully, navigating dire situations with courage and wisdom.

John Calvin takes a literal reading of Psalm 8 to argue that children are examples of faith and participants in God's covenant.[11] In the Exodus account, Yahweh makes powerful statements connecting the freeing of the Israelites with the worship of the people, including children. The imperative, "Let my son go that he may worship me" (Exod 4:23 and 9:1), elevates both the work of worship and the need for all to contribute. Parents' willingness to give the child *back* to God (e.g., the sacrifice of Isaac, the committing of Samson to God's service) offer powerful examples of God using children and youth to advance the covenant and faith of Israel.

Children also exemplify faithfulness themselves. This quality leads Old Testament scholar Esther Menn to lament the fact that children are too often overlooked and neglected in serious biblical interpretation. David, Joseph, Rebekah, Miriam, Samuel, the Israelite servant girl, and Jephthah's daughter are a few examples of young people deserving of scholarly attention.[12] New Testament experts and theologians such as Judith Gundry and Joyce Ann Mercer show the ways that children model faithfulness through discipleship.[13] Further work on children's participation in God's kingdom would provide paradigms for Christians to think through the vocation of children in specific and varied ways.

---

10. Gelman, *Queen Esther*.

11. Miller-McLemore, "Jesus Loves the Little Children?," 9.

12. Menn, "Child Characters in Biblical Narratives," 324.

13. See Mercer, *Welcoming Children*, and Gundry-Volf, "The Least and the Greatest."

In addition to individual characters in the biblical narrative, children are the loci of broad generational flourishing and are valued as the ones through whom Israel sustains memory, stories, ethos, and rituals. Patrick Miller, professor of Old Testament studies, notes that participating in cultic activities, such as worship, is a crucial way for children to learn.[14] The attention given to their learning and formation assumes that children are valued as actors in Israel's story, and as such, they are important transporters of memory. In Deuteronomy and the wisdom literature, Scripture gives explicit attention to children's formation and discipline. Discipline is not confined to correcting bad behavior but is used in the constructive sense, for discipline grows faithful followers of Yahweh. The word *discipline* is the root of discipleship, and the development in the texts underscores the etymological connection. Miller argues that teaching in Deuteronomy aims to form children in the story.[15] It is not enough for them to learn the rules. They need to be involved in the rituals and practices that reveal the larger picture of God's activity and relationship with Israel.

For example, Deuteronomy 16 indicates two festivals in which children—including sons, daughters, and orphans—are participants. *Shavout*, the festival of weeks, and *Sukkot*, the festival of booths, underscore the reasons. Together, they ritualize decisive moments in Israel's story—God giving Israelites the Torah, the first fruits of the harvest, the exodus from Egypt, and the way of life before the Promised Land. Through song, dance, music, and food, the rituals convey the very thing Queen Esther fought to preserve—the lived reality behind Israel's commandments and guidelines. When children learn and live in the story and its rituals, they absorb meaning on the level of identity and character.[16]

Proverbs is another example in which the child's discipline and education occur over the long haul, and the narrative gives the process much attention.[17] Education is connected with growth and maturation. While the hope is that all continue to grow in Christ, more often the capacity to learn, grow, and mature is linked with children. In this way, their roles as learners

14. Miller, "That the Children May Know," 45.

15. Ibid.

16. Ibid., 50. For a broad survey of children in religion, see Browning and Miller-McLemore, eds., *Children and Childhood in American Religions*. Jennifer Beste has a particularly worthwhile chapter on children in Judaism.

17. Brown, "To Discipline without Destruction," 63–81.

and growers bestow an invaluable word to the community of faith, and they become strong participants in the covenantal and relational aspects of faith.

In the New Testament, children are valued as members of the body of Christ and participate in the body by using their gifts. All those who are baptized—whether male, female, young or old—are a part of the body (1 Cor 12). The Apostle Paul's theology of baptism levels the playing field as he exhorts his congregations not to privilege one member and his or her gifts over another's. Beverly Roberts Gaventa discusses how this is applied to worship in 1 Corinthians 14. Paul desires that all members use their gifts, and that none should overshadow or mute another.[18] Gaventa suggests that the utilization of gifts is a provocative idea when applied to children. Of Paul's understanding of the unity of the body in light of gifts, she writes,

> ...it is important also to reflect on the roles children occupy in the body of Christ or in the household of God. What gifts do children bring to that body, gifts that often go unnoticed? Perhaps the most obvious gift is the gift of love, since it is in receiving and being received by children that many parents (and not only parents) find their capacity for love enlarged past all imagining. Children also contribute to the human capacity for doxology and wonder. . . . While these may be the contributions of the "weaker" members of the body, they are by no means negligible.[19]

We revisit children's capacities for love and wonder and develop children's vocation in Christ's church in chapters 4 and 5, but presently we call attention to children's contributions such as those Gaventa names and as they are embedded in Pauline ecclesiology. Children's gifts may be small, but they are not negligible, and moreover, God works through their gifts and blesses the whole.

Children: Blessed Signs

John refers to believers as God's children. "See what love the Father has given us, that we should be called children of God; and that is what we are" (1 John 3:1). "Children of God" refers to both adults and children alike. Scripture's widespread use of the child or children as a trope contributes additional theological dimensions for understanding children, their place in the kingdom, and God's relationship to humanity. The prevalence of the

18. Gaventa, "Finding a Place for Children," 246.

19. Ibid., 247.

interconnected themes such as God as parent, children of God, becoming like a child, and other metaphorical references to children link the category of children to actual children and their import in God's work of salvation. Clement of Alexandria's *Paedagogus* develops the ways that childhood is a dominant theme, describing what it means to grow in faith and averring that all Christians are in some ways children.[20] These themes stand out in biblical writers' use of child or children to describe Israel and her relationship to Yahweh. Paul's letters also contain significant metaphorical developments of the child, and the New Testament as a whole contains references to fictive familial relationships within the community God calls and gathers. Moreover, the use of children as a metaphor is closely related to the metaphor of adoption that the biblical narrative develops as a description of how humanity becomes linked to Christ.

Israel: Child of God

The metaphor of Israel as God's child is profound in the Old Testament. Old Testament scholar Jacqueline Lapsley unpacks the purpose and meaning of the trope. She offers two critical aspects for the discussion. First, she addresses the actual children in Isaiah, including both familiar, named children, as well as the more vulnerable orphans. Her analysis of actual children provides depth to the use of the child as a trope, and interpreting this second aspect of Israel as child relies on the characteristics of the actual child. Through the naming of the prophet Isaiah's children, God communicates his purposes to Israel. The children (Shear-jashub, Immanuel, and Maher-shalal-hash-baz) are the loci for God's sign-acts conveying judgement and hope through the children themselves. The names communicate that a remnant shall return, that God is with us, and that pillage hastens.[21] These names communicate comfort but also judgement. Israel is in need of God and has not been entirely faithful, and the children transmit the truth of Israel's status with God.

While it appears that these names are merely signs of something larger, it is also true that particular children have value and import in Isaiah. Children pair with widows as the most vulnerable members of society, and Isaiah speaks about injustices toward them as signals of a society's

20. See especially Book I of the *Paedagogus* in Clement's *Christ the Educator* for his development of Christian formation.

21. Lapsley, "Look!," 83–84.

unfaithfulness, meriting God's judgement. Orphaned children have rights, and the Torah seeks to protect their welfare. Lapsley notes that the Torah develops protection by addressing the responsibilities of people and groups in power. God clearly cares about the plight of children, especially orphaned ones, and their centrality to the law is powerful. As such, one can say much about Israel's broader relationship with Yahweh. If she is not responding to her weakest and most vulnerable members, it is likely that Israel is not attuned to other aspects of the law.[22]

Beyond simply revealing how children are treated in the present life, Isaiah depicts images of children in the eschaton to contrast how children are supposed to be incorporated with how they are actually being treated. Lapsley notes the injunctions against Israel in the very first chapter. First, they are not attending to the welfare of orphans (Isa 1:23). She notes how the accusations build and in chapter 10, Israel is described as taking orphans as prey. In contrast, Lapsely points out the hopeful images of the future. These include the promise of a son, the peaceful image of the (prey) child who tends to the (predator) wolf, and the vision of children playing without fear.[23] Isaiah's eschatological vision of God's peace culminates in chapter 65 with the new heavens and earth as a place where no child or infant will die an early death. Thus, in these texts, children are "intimately bound up with both the judgement of Israel and the promise of deliverance."[24]

God cares for actual children, and Isaiah employs God's heart for children as a trope for Israel herself as God's child. Building on the ways that children are agents of promise and loci for judgment, Isaiah offers many images that round out the parent-child relationship between Yahweh and Israel. She is a rebellious child in need of discipline and daughter Zion who will not be abandoned. She is called by name and she is ultimately incorporated by adoption.

Christians: Children of God

New Testament references to children, particularly in Paul, focus on themes that echo those pertaining to Israel in the Old Testament. The Christian's identity as a child of God and the notion that Christians are heirs of the kingdom resonate well with Israel's own relationship with Yahweh. In both,

22 Ibid., 83, 86.
23 Ibid., 87, 90.
24 Ibid., 91.

kinship structure and fictive families are stabilizing structures through which humans establish roles, live out their faith, and grow in relationship to God.

One of the more striking texts is Matthew's on inheriting the kingdom: "Truly I tell you, unless you change and become like children, you will never enter the kingdom of heaven" (Matt 18:3). Matthew's telling of the story focuses not on Jesus' own actions but on the drama of the disciples, specifically on their own formation. The positive call and constructive message of this text comes in the language of a distinctive practice—"change and become." The mark of transformation worthy of inheritance is that of being "like children." Transformation in which one is like a child, then, carries weight in the saving work of God. Become small to participate in the big.

Mark's gospel also uses this saying of Jesus to indicate how we become heirs of God's kingdom. In contrast to Matthew's Gospel, Mark places emphasis on the kingdom as belonging to those in need—and children are at the top of the list. As Judith Gundry notes, the Greek construction of Mark 10:14—"it is to such as these [children] that the kingdom belongs"—is in the genitive form denoting possession.[25] The kingdom belongs to children. Gundry argues that the kingdom belongs to those who need it, such as sinners and tax collectors. Children are in most need not because they are the greatest sinners, but rather because they are objectively dependent on God.[26] Hence, children's dependence foregrounds the notion that they are heirs of the kingdom.

Dependence is the first aspect of one's willingness to receive grace, and Paul similarly discusses the child as a metaphor for formation (e.g., Rom 8:14–17), developing this notion in the context of the Christian church. In Paul's writing the metaphor of the child connotes the lengthy process of maturing in faith. He uses parent and child metaphors to describe the body's relationship to God and the body's relationship to Paul himself. First Corinthians notes that members ought to imitate Paul so that they might become mature like Paul (1 Cor 2–3). As theologian and philosopher Reidar Aasgaard observes, Paul shows concern and care for his Corinthian children and treats them according to their abilities and capacities, honoring the time it takes to develop them.[27]

25. Gundry, "Children in the Gospel of Mark," 151.

26. Ibid., 152.

27. Aasgaard, "Like a Child," 273.

An additional descriptor that Paul often employs is "beloved." Paul takes great care in detailing the meaning of beloved, and in particular, through the role of a mother in relation to her child. He identifies both with the role of mother and with the idea of being the recipient of a mother's love. Paul describes the people of Corinth as babies in need of breast milk. He calls Timothy a "beloved and faithful child" and in his first letter to the Thessalonians, he uses tender images of a mother caring for her child (1 Thess 2:7). Paul also references the experience of being cared for himself by the mother of Rufus (Rom 16:13).[28] The ways in which he links beloved and child deepen the inherent value of the category "child" and its place in the community's relationship to one another and to God.

Such care demonstrates the personal connection Paul has with his churches. He sees them for what they are—at times young, immature, and vulnerable in faith. Instead of cutting them off or moving on to more capable, mature communities, Paul remains committed to his churches just as good parents are committed to their own children. He encourages the churches to participate. He watches them fail. He encourages them to keep striving and to persevere in the race they are called to run. Paul's intense and direct comments via his letters show that he takes his churches seriously and desires for them to grow. Paul clearly recognizes, as Aasgaard notes, that childhood is a phase of life, and he uses the category to show the importance of Christian formation in its earliest phases.

Incorporation & Adoption

Scripture characterizes God's incorporating activity through the theological category of adoption, advancing the place of both the actual child and the metaphorical child in God's drama. While incorporation constitutes the heart of chapter 3, we address it here through Jesus' incorporation of children. Adoption is another key category marking humans as part of God's life. Christian ethicist Amy Laura Hall argues that adoption is *the* mode by which all people, including adults, become children of God.[29] The theme of adoption resonates deeply with the actual situation of children and especially of the orphan. This is true both because children are the ones who are adopted, and because adoption is the process of choosing or initiating—an event of full belonging or salvation.

28. Ibid., 263–65.

29. Hall, *Conceiving Parenthood*, 394.

In Mark's Gospel, two aforementioned texts especially highlight the centrality of children for God. In Mark 9:36, Jesus calls the disciples to him as he takes a little child into his arms. At the same time, Jesus offers an interpretation of his own actions: "Whoever welcomes one such child in my name welcomes me" (Mark 9:37). A number of aspects in this pericope are striking. First, Jesus enacts the truth that he conveys. He does not simply command the disciples to welcome children, he literally *receives* a child into his arms.

The visual image of Jesus humbling himself in the face of a child—in contrast with the disciples' previous disputes over who among them was greatest—must have struck a note of surprise, if not obeisance, among the twelve. Jesus practices what he preaches, even with the powerless, and in doing so behaves counterculturally. Joyce Ann Mercer points out that using the words *receive* or *welcome* offer an occasion for Jesus to highlight the dependence of the disciples in their own vocations of preaching the coming kingdom.[30] She concludes that the child in Jesus' arms creates a teaching moment to demonstrate a radical social reordering that is God's kingdom.[31] The one who is not a person in the eyes of the Roman Empire (and quite likely the disciples) sits in solidarity with the Messiah at Jesus' invitation.

Next, Jesus *identifies* with the children through his statement, which is noticeably similar to his identification with the vulnerable in the parable of the sheep and the goats in Matthew 25. Jesus tells the disciples that in welcoming a child, one welcomes Jesus himself. While Jesus' affinity with the little child is significant, the clause that follows is more salient: "…and whoever welcomes me welcomes not only me but the one who sent me" (Mark 9:37), referring to the Father. Such a pronouncement links the twofold identification of Jesus with the child on the one hand and with the Father on the other.

This significant scene demonstrates the importance of children, the way Jesus deals with power in unique and countercultural ways, and the *telos* of discipleship—welcoming and incorporating all. By linking this *telos* with the judgment in Matthew 25, Jesus' words are further underscored. God's kingdom is about the least of these, and children represent both the content and the way of this unusual kingdom.

While the imagery resonates with the incorporating activity of Father, Son, and Holy Spirit, Paul uses the language of adoption to develop the new

30. Mercer, *Welcoming Children*, 51.
31. Ibid.

creature's life in Christ. In Romans, he speaks of adoption both as a present reality and as an eschatological future. He refers both to Gentiles and to Israel as being adopted. Romans 8:15 exhorts persons to live according to Spirit, and all who call God "Abba" to bear witness that they are children of God. The Spirit they receive is the Spirit of adoption and the way in which persons become heirs of Jesus Christ. Later, in verse 23, Paul speaks of the "not yet" of the Spirit of adoption. God's people and, in fact, all of creation await the redemption of the body. Redemption, or incorporation, marks the future hope and promise of adoption. Romans 9 advances the discussion in terms of Israel's own adoption. Adoption, writes Paul, belongs to Israel, along with the glory of God's covenants, the giving of the law, worship, and the promises.

In his letter to the Galatians, Paul contrasts Gentile incorporation into Christ with Jewish incorporation through the law. Gentiles, Paul indicates, come to adoption through faith. In chapters 4–6, the linking, or adoptive, work of the Spirit happens at many levels. First, Paul (as parent) links the church in Galatia (as children) to himself. He begs them to become as he is. Since the church members welcome him as an "angel of God" (Gal 4:14), Paul is able to incorporate them through the language of childbirth and parenting. As with Paul's sentiments toward other churches, he will not leave the Galatians.

Paul also links the Galatians to one another. In Galatians 6, he calls them to bear one another's burdens (6:2) and to share in the good of all, especially those in the family of faith (6:10). Shortly before he uses the language of adoption, he tells the Galatians that through faith they are one in Christ Jesus. In other words, not only are they linked with one another, they are linked with one another *through* Christ.

In all of this, he attributes the "linking" work to the activity of the Spirit. Sowing the Spirit reaps eternal life, and the same Spirit that works in Jesus' own adoption in baptism works in the adoption of the Gentiles. The Spirit's work of linking is associated with fruit, new creation, and Jesus Christ. In 4:4–7, Paul writes,

> But when the fullness of time had come, God sent his Son, born of a woman, born under the law, in order to redeem those who were under the law, so that we might receive adoption as children. And because you are children, God has sent the Spirit of his Son into our hearts, crying, "Abba! Father!" So you are no longer a slave but a child, and if a child then also an heir, through God.

This passage beautifully expresses adoption in the context of trinitarian incorporation and explicitly connects children and adoption with the Spirit's activity.

Jesus' incorporation of actual children and the metaphorical development of children of God as adopted describe God's redemptive work of salvation. Metaphors only go so far. Yet they convey deep truths that literal descriptions cannot, and moreover, they are connected to the actual referent. If the faith community does not understand the basic categories used in constructing the central metaphors—in this case child, children, and adoption—then its understanding of God and ability to relate to God are truncated. In sum, the prevalence and power of children reveal what it means to be heirs of the kingdom of God. Children participate in and represent ways that people are incorporated into God's triune family, supporting our thesis that children are central to understanding the Spirit's activity of linking the church to Christ.

The Good News of the Child

The particular children in Scripture and the trope of the child and childhood offer powerful ways that God does big work in and through the small. However, this raises a critical theological question: how? How does the Spirit make way for Isaac in a senescent Sarah? Why is the first king of Israel chosen from the smallest tribe of Benjamin? How does God make mountain-moving faith out of a mustard seed? Why do doves and lambs take center stage in John's proclamation of salvation? The creedal answer is that God creates from nothing. But there is something more. The overall trajectory of the biblical narrative reveals a God who reverses the economy of the small, and the truth underlying young Brooke's ecclesiology is that our very big God comes to us in a small form. God reverses the order of power and limits his big, transcendent, all-powerful divinity to become an infant.

Reading Scripture as a whole allows readers to experience the development of themes over time, which often leads to surprises. For example, God reveals God's triune nature in the Old Testament through the differentiation of beings, such as word/wisdom, spirit, and creator. God breaks into the created world through signs, such as the burning bush, and through voice, in the instances of Hagar and Samuel. The differentiation of persons within God and the incarnate manifestations in the Old Testament build toward the full revelation of God in the New Testament. God takes on human form.

Similarly, the place of the child and the trope of children move toward a revelation. In the Old Testament, children play central roles at various points in the plot. The prophets' message to care for orphans is repetitive and forceful. The strength of Israel's relationship with God is in no small way determined by how it cares for children—not only for her own, but for all children. In the New Testament, Jesus heals children and tends to them in ways that are confusing to adults. Paul also recognizes the children among them, but more frequently, he uses the metaphor of children as the very way humans are adopted into God's triune community. In the middle of this trajectory of salvation through adoption, God becomes the child— the child whom Isaiah describes as Emmanuel, God with us.

A Child Is Born

We offer two points to advance the significance of the child in God's kingdom through an examination of Christ-as-Child. The first point is that God actually becomes small, as noted above. God intentionally limits his power and transcendence and takes the form of a human *first through an infant*. God does not bypass these early stages but rather takes on the utter vulnerability that is pronounced in childhood—an idea that is made expressly clear in non-canonical witnesses, such as the Infancy Gospel of Thomas.[32] The second is that God as child relates to a human mother and divine Father, and in this way, the category of child refers once again to the Spirit's work of linking the body, or the church, to Christ.

The significance of the baby and the Christ-child are framed in Scripture, not least through the accounts of the barren women and Isaiah. Throughout the Old Testament, key matriarchs in Israel's history experience barrenness and cry out to God for a child. Sarah, Rebekah, Rachel, and Hannah all suffer in their childlessness. God eventually answers them, giving each one the gift of children, and these children participate in God's story in ways that are integral to Israel's salvation. In the New Testament, Elizabeth's barrenness opens up the story for the virgin birth, and God becomes a child in and through the genealogy of barrenness. Humanity is

---

32. Aasgaard, *The Childhood of Jesus*, 157. Aasgaard asserts that the Infancy Gospel of Thomas makes it clear that Jesus is fully human and fully divine by emphasizing that he is "true God and true child."

created time and again from nothing, as barrenness makes way for children and, ultimately, for the Child. Second Isaiah crystallizes this theological point through the use of childlessness to pave the way for God's redemption of Israel (Isa 54).[33] Scripture recurrently links the presence and absence of children with the story's acknowledgment that the gift of children is from God alone. In the midst of Israel recognizing the gift of the child, God himself becomes a child and advances God's kingdom to the point of redemption. The Child, in other words, becomes the redemptive gift to all humanity, or servant of the Lord, as Second Isaiah proclaims.

Isaiah also foretells the Christ as a child explicitly. He describes the Messiah in both powerful and child-like terms. On the one hand, the Messiah is named "Wonderful Counselor, Mighty God, Everlasting Father, Prince of Peace" (Isa 9:6). Authority rests on him, and he will establish a kingdom of justice and righteousness. On the other hand, the one who establishes the kingdom and on whose shoulders authority rests is none other than a child. Isaiah's prediction reads, "For a *child* has been *born* for us, a son given to us" (Isa 9:6, italics added). Not only is the child the central actor of God's saving work, but his first action, birth, becomes the leading theological metaphor for understanding the believer's entrance into God's kingdom. A child is born, for the new birth of humanity.

Birth is paramount. Luke's gospel takes eighty verses to prepare readers for the birth and then another fifty-two on his infancy, naming, presentation, and formation before moving on to his baptism. Clearly, Luke finds infancy and childhood significant. His detail and attention further illumines the unusual presence of God as a child.

A Son Is Given

The second point emphasizing the place of the child through God's taking on the form of a child is his relationship with his mother and his Father. His earthly father, Joseph, also plays a role in Jesus' formation and development as a child. Accounts of Mary and Joseph's relationship are more prominent in the Infancy Gospel of Thomas, where Joseph is portrayed as an involved parent, than in the canonical Gospels.[34] However, for our purposes of showing the child as a category that brings together the divine

33. For more on this, see Michelle Clifton-Soderstrom, "Beyond the Blessed/Cursed Dichotomy."

34. Aasgaard, *The Childhood of Jesus*, 109–10.

and human as part of salvation, we focus on Jesus' relationship with Mary and with his heavenly Father.

Catholics stand out in their theology celebrating the place of Jesus' mother in saving history. While Scripture provides few details of Jesus and Mary's relationship, it is important to note that the two shared love and that Jesus allowed himself to be her child. Perhaps this is depicted nowhere better than in Michelangelo's *Pietà*. In this stunning sculpture, Michelangelo at once portrays the intimacy and the power of the child Jesus lying dead in his mother's arms. Its accuracy and truth is compelling, both in the love with which Mary's body surrounds that of her son's as well as in Jesus' absolute surrender, even unto death. In her grief, Mary's left hand lays open and extended as if inviting the viewer into the death. Her gesture amends the scene, and resurrection hope comes in the form of incorporating others into their intimate relationship. The prominence of Michelangelo's masterpiece fits the truth that sonship and relationship matter in the story of salvation, and in fact are the pathway to communion with the divine.

Jesus' sonship was *as* human. The Council of Ephesus (431) affirmed that Jesus was so fully Mary's son that Mary is the *theotokos*, or the Mother of God. The focus of the Council's claims was primarily Christological in that it affirmed the unity of the divine and human natures of Christ. In other words, the divine nature of God unites with humanity in the being of a child. The quality of sonship frames the aspect of child that is Jesus, and while scholars disagree on the meaning of the term "Son of Man," the early church Fathers believed that it referred to his being the Son of a human, namely of Mary.

Jesus was also the Son of God, and throughout the Gospel narratives Jesus continues to mark his identity as God's Son. The Gospels and Paul cooperatively reveal God and the Son's relationship as having saving power. Over and over again, Jesus refers to the Father in regard to his will, goodness, justice, and plans. These plans are not limited to Jesus but are for all humanity and creation as a whole.

Gospel readers become aware of Jesus' relationship to his Father at the beginning of all four accounts.[35] In the story of Jesus' baptism, the dove descends and the voice calls out, "This is my Son with whom I am well

35. In referring to the Father, it is easy to think that God has a gender. We categorically reject that God has the gender of man and instead direct readers to the language that Jesus and the Gospels use to denote a particular aspect of the relationship of the two persons of the Trinity. We argue from Genesis 1:27 that God's being encompasses both genders as they are made in God's image.

pleased." It is a reconciliation moment, a word about God's atoning love, even before Jesus has done an ounce of ministry. In a theological sense, it is almost as if Jesus is born again. It is certainly the case that readers become explicitly aware for the first time that Jesus is God's Son and that identity matters.

The significance of the relationship of Son to Father is marked in John the Baptist's words, "Here is the Lamb of God who takes away the sin of the world!" (John 1:29). When connected with the saving statement of John the Baptist, the divine aspect of the sonship of Jesus is revealed. Not only is Jesus son of a human, Jesus is also Son of God, and in both truths the actual and ritualistic dimensions of birth are present. The child is a category through which human and divine are brought together for the work of salvation.

Roman Catholics often wear the blessed *Agnus Dei* (Lamb of God) around their necks, especially during Easter. Made from the wax of the previous year's Paschal candle, the *Agnus Dei* is impressed with a lamb (usually with a cross) on one side and another figure, such as a saint, on the other. They can be worn or they can simply be objects that help believers pray. *Agnus Deis* hold special meaning, not unlike the crosses that Protestants wear, because they remind people of the unity that is the divine and human nature of Christ. The liturgy incorporates the *Agnus Dei* three times in preparation for communion, the sacrament of peace and unity. This unity is real in the Incarnation of Christ, and its power, as John reveals, is saving. In other words, the Child of God is the sacrament that takes away the sin of the world.

Through the category of child and the reality that Jesus was both Son of Man and Son of God, God saves. The big becomes small, and God blesses it and makes it big. Scripture, the creeds, and all the sacraments bespeak God's unusual economy of blessing. As it reflects Christ, the church's work of incorporating the small habituates the body to see God in the small and ushers in the possibility that children are indeed coworkers in advancing God's kingdom on earth. Every little bit counts in God's economy of grace.

Conclusion

Baptisms are small events. They acknowledge beginnings, not endings. Jesus was baptized before he began his formal ministry, yet rarely is his baptism a moment that Christians recall when they think of God's big, saving acts. Finding the big in the small is difficult. Is something big really happening in the small event of an earthly baptism? Will God's grace really take hold? Is this person ready for what lies ahead? One wonders how the ritual has remained central for 2,000 years of church history.

Yet we continue the liturgy, pray over the water, and take our vows to care and nurture each baptizand who graces our worship. While we may not be cognizant of all God is doing, the church preserves the sacrament because it remains hopeful that God is doing big things in the small. Baptism celebrates the small yet big work that God is doing, called new creation. For each congregation who reads this book, we hope that your congregation aspires to be as big for the world as Brooke's small church is for her. The good news is that together we are big through the power of the Father, and the Child, and the Holy Spirit.

Children
Worship
Incorporation
Virtue
Vocation
Vision

2. Worship

About a year ago, my (Dave's) pastor Aaron and his spouse, Lenore, were home with their then three-year-old son Elijah. Aaron and his family had recently been out on a pastoral visit with a congregant who had major surgery and was homebound for the next few months. An integral part of the visit was the reception of communion, which Aaron transported using a small portable communion set (which I can verify works better than putting cellophane over the mouth of the cup, placing it in your car's cup holder, and driving down the pothole-ridden streets of Chicago!). The communion set was still out on a table, and Elijah became entranced by this clasped box with its interior cups and cavities. Soon he was busy opening and closing the box, organizing the small cups, and playing the self-directed games whose function and rules are only discernible within the world of a child. When Lenore saw Elijah's game, she was torn as to the proper parental response. Should she stop Elijah from playing with these holy elements, to prevent him from thinking of communion as a game? Or would that give the impression that communion was something so holy that it edged on the fearful, the out-of-bounds, and thus create negative connotations with communion and, indirectly, God? As she was deciding what to do, Elijah's game slowed. He raised his curly head and declared, "Come and taste this grace!" In Elijah's simple declaration, Lenore's questions were answered in the grace presented by her son. And a little child shall lead them.

At Resurrection Covenant Church in Chicago, we receive communion every week, so it is not surprising that Elijah wanted to play communion. We believe that communion is not only a normative part of the worship of the early church as witnessed in the biblical account (Acts 2:42, 20:7; 1 Cor 11:20)—it also encapsulates the great story of God. Communion celebrates a God who gave his own Son by the power of the Holy Spirit so that we may unite with our brothers and sisters around the bread and cup. Communion supplies the sustenance to live out the vision of God's triune life in the world where all who hunger and thirst are filled, systems of oppressive hierarchy are overthrown, and all find true community in the body of Christ. Each week, our pastor invites the congregation into the liturgy, and after passing the elements to the servers, he looks out into the congregation, raises his hands, and invites us: "The table is set; all is ready. Come and taste grace."

One could argue that Elijah was simply mimicking what he had seen his dad say and do countless times on Sunday mornings. To be sure, Elijah could not possibly understand the full ramifications of communion, the 2,000 years of controversies, the denominations that have been formed and splintered debating over what exactly happens to the elements at the table. Yet it is also true that none of us understands the elements. None of us can pinpoint how grace infuses our lives and suffuses our communities through the simple elements of bread and wine. None of us fully grasps God's great and gracious descent into our midst. During the Eucharistic controversies of the Reformation, John Calvin admitted, "Now if anyone should ask me how this takes place, I shall not be ashamed to confess that it is a secret too lofty for either the mind to comprehend or my words to declare. . . . I rather experience than understand it."[1] As with the rest of us, John Calvin included, young Elijah does not fully understand, but he experiences—and he leads.

In the case of children, experiencing worship offers building blocks—small and incomplete parts and pieces of seemingly little value. It may come in the form of simple words such as, "Come and taste grace," or the refrain of a hymn, "Great is thy faithfulness, Lord, unto me." Possibly, it comes in the form of ritual actions such as the passing of the peace with our neighbors or lifting our hands palms up to receive the final benediction. Christian ethicist Jennifer Beste offers quantitative research on second graders' experiences of the sacrament of reconciliation. Through the categories of affective response, meaningfulness, and impact on relationship

1. Calvin, *Institutes*, 4.17.32.

with God, Beste notes a diversity of responses. She concludes, though, that overall children actively construct meaning and have the ability to respond creatively.[2] In other words, they are not simply empty vessels to be filled. Moreover, she found that in contrast to adults, children responded to the sacrament with "joy and radical openness to experiencing God's love."[3] Her work underscores the significance of children's participation in each of the worship parts.

With these building blocks, children continually construct meaning out of the apparent chaos of the world. As children grow in their faith, these building blocks often serve as a foundation of that faith. This is why it is crucial that the church saturates our services with words of abiding meaning, prayers of worthy construction, and songs of truth and beauty—not simply the popular and disposable. Our stories of God must be built with elements of enduring and lasting value rather than the superficial and transient. Similarly, by maintaining a few stable ritual elements in worship that serve as landmarks and constants, we make space for children to interact with common elements over long periods of time, intentionally fostering their faith formation. Children may not grasp the fullness of every symbol and act of worship, but those symbols and structures of worship create the constructs from which children understand themselves, their world, and their God. Worship is the place for faith in the making.

Worship: What It Is and Why It Matters

One of the dangers of writing a book about integrating children into the worshiping life of the church is the temptation to jump headlong into the nature of children or tips and strategies for including children in worship before thinking critically about what worship is and why children matter to a worshiping community. Indeed, well-meaning churches, pastors, and children's directors have often launched initiatives to include children in worship and ended up doing so at the expense of both. Children become mere tokens of cuteness or the means to a good laugh during the children's sermon, thus depriving them of their dignity and worth as true worshipers of Christ. Worship loses its direction and purpose when children's sermons, choirs, or dramas are haphazardly added without thought to the goals of worship. With these cautions in mind, this chapter begins with

2. Beste, "Children Speak," 346.
3. Ibid., 347.

two fundamental questions: 1) What is worship? and 2) Why do children matter in the worshiping life of the church?

Worship is a word that carries a host of meanings and overtones depending on the context and company. Outside of the church, worship can connote anything from the highest praise of a band or celebrity (i.e., "He worships the Beatles!") to the dark and fear-inducing sacrificial rituals of modern-day pagan cults and anything in between these poles of banality and fright. Even within the confines of the Christian church, worship can describe the silent meeting of the Quaker, the incense and icons of the Orthodox, the simple chant of the monastics, or the ecstasy and spontaneity of the charismatics. Worship left undefined can mean a myriad of things, many of which hold little or no reference to the biblical or historic witness of Christian worship.

For the purposes of this book, we are defining Christian worship as the enactment of the dramatic story of the triune God by the people of God. Such a definition reminds us that worship is: 1) primarily God-centered, 2) dialogical, 3) enacted, 4) storied, and 5) practiced by the people of God—the church. This definition provides boundary markers that help describe Christian worship, allowing us to move forward into a larger discussion about the role children should play within it. But first, let us unpack each of these characteristics of Christian worship so that we might explore more fully what Christian worship is and what it is not.

Worship Is God-Centered

Christian worship is centered on the glorification of God. Whatever other concerns we may have about worship—accessibility of the liturgy, singability of songs, building aesthetics, beauty of language—all find their proper secondary place in reference to the primary object of worship: the triune God.[4] The triune God is the God who creates the world and continues to be faithful even when we are not. Ours is the God who called forth the Hebrew people to be God's people and a light to all nations, the God who sent God's Son into the world to live, die, and be raised for the sake of the entire universe, the God who poured out the Holy Spirit at Pentecost and established the church, the God who promises to come once more and establish God's

---

4. In the classic trinitarian understanding of worship, God is both subject and object of worship as Christ intercedes to the Father on our behalf through the power of the Holy Spirit.

kingdom "on earth as it is in heaven." The only proper response to this God is pure and undivided worship in which God "must increase, but I must decrease" (John 3:30).

The idea that God is the center of worship in many ways plays against our tendencies to make worship primarily about us. Anthropocentric, or human-centered, worship is characterized by songs that overemphasize "I" and "me" language or make petitions the end of prayer. Human-centered worship is critical of style or defines a successful Sunday if the sermon "speaks to me" or the songs "help me feel worshipful." Human-centered worship may even come in the form of catering worship to seekers in a way that neglects the diversity of Christians in the body. After all, worship that sells and succeeds must keep its eye on what is relevant!

When people gather to worship, it is definitively Christian when God is the center, the source, the arbiter, the means, and the end of all the worship and the liturgical choices we make. Old Testament scholar James Bruckner writes about Eden in terms of blessing and worship. Eden is the bounded place where each lives according to its kind, and God blesses these patterns of relations, calling them good. In Eden, God has set up boundaries for the completion of God's creative work. The creative work, according to Bruckner, is defined in the midst of Adam's relationship to God, and Bruckner calls this work "worship."[5] Worship is the center boundary of the Garden of Eden and the expression of what human beings were created for—glorifying God.

After humans transgress the boundaries that God has set, God replaces the garden with the temple. The temple becomes the sacred place marking the ongoing creative relationship between God and human beings. The temple is "the place of worship, submission and transformation."[6] Describing the way of the temple, Bruckner notes that Jewish studies scholar Jon Levenson calls it a new place of existence characterized by intimacy with God, a true paradise, and an ascent in which worshipers through liturgy find the fullness of what it means to be created in the image of God.

When worship is centered on God, children find their place in worship alongside the adults in the congregation, for the ends and purposes are bigger than either group alone. Together, the congregation grows into what it means to be created in God's image. If worship is not under pressure to create a perfect atmosphere of peace and tranquility in order for adults

5. Bruckner, "Boundary and Freedom," 15–35.
6. Ibid., 18.

to feel God, then children will no longer be seen as nuisances to put up with or distractions that must be ushered out of the sanctuary during the serious parts of the service. Worship is not about the wishes and desires of any one contingent within the congregation, no matter their class, size, sex, or ability to tithe. Worship centered on God puts all people—children, adults, elderly, the mentally or physically disabled—on equal footing before the presence of an encompassing God. Children may be treated like every other worshiper as full participants who bring their praise and adoration to God. If we understand worship as primarily about God, our conversation then shifts from asking what to do with children during worship to how we can rid ourselves of barriers that prevent children, or anyone for that matter, from bringing their unique voice and gifts to God and the church.

Worship Is Dialogical

"Eden is a conversation," asserts nature writer Barry Lopez, referring to the dialogue between human beings and God that occurs in the midst of good relations, scrupulously attended to and imaginatively maintained.[7] Lopez further describes Eden conversations as an exercise of love for one another. Eden conversations serve as a divestiture from our sense of self-importance and evoke openness to the divine. From Eden to the temple and beyond, worship as dialogue with God grows relationships. Worship is the place where Christians have their conversations with God, exercise love for one another, and imaginatively maintain good relations.

When the praise of God is the central aspect of worship, worship is truly dialogical. Throughout the liturgy, the congregation hears God speak and responds to God's word through the various means of adoration, confession, lament, thanksgiving, intercession, and obedience. Worship draws persons into the presence of a holy God, where it is possible for worshipers to realize—like Adam and Eve—that the rags one uses to cover up brokenness and sin are useless before the God who sees. In the presence of God, the people cry with the prophet Isaiah: "Woe is me! I am a person of unclean lips, and I live among a people of unclean lips; yet my eyes have seen the King, the Lord of hosts!" (Isa 6:5). And the wonder of the Christian faith is encapsulated in the words of assurance—the reminder that in spite of all-encompassing sin, the God of the universe condescends to humanity and lives, dies, and is risen among us so that we might be redeemed. Upon

7. Lopez, "Eden Is a Conversation."

hearing these words of unmatched and unmerited grace, the congregation responds through acclamations of adoration and praise:

> No condemnation now I dread,
> Jesus, and all in him, is mine;
> Alive in him, my living Head
> And clothed in righteousness divine!
> Bold I approach the eternal throne
> And claim the crown through Christ my own!
> Amazing love! How can it be
> that thou my God shouldst die for me?[8]

In worship, the body also hears the words of God's redemption and questions how such love and peace can be true in a world that seems firmly held captive by the powers of oppression, sickness, and violence of every kind. When God's promises collide with the world's realities, worshipers cry with the psalmist, "How long, O Lord?" In these words, we bring our raw and unedited lament to God, assured that God hears the cries of the faithful and will bring about transformation. Similarly, we respond to the brokenness in the world by interceding on its behalf and beseeching God to bring about healing and redemption.

Finally, Christians hear God's word spoken in worship and respond through obedience and a life lived in response to God's grace and in the light of God's kingdom. Sendings charge the faithful to go into our world and live out the "liturgy after the liturgy" (as the Orthodox are fond of saying)—taking the precepts of praise of God and responding with a life of obedience as the truest form of worship. We answer God's "Whom shall I send?" with a corporate "Here we are—send us!" It is then we realize that all life is worship; it is an attuning of ourselves to the ever-speaking voice of God in the seemingly trivial and mundane of the world and responding to this voice with a resounding "Amen! So be it!"—a cry that demands our lives be conformed and transformed into a living, moving, and breathing doxology to the living God.

Worship as dialogue assumes that God speaks to God's people and calls forth a response from the whole body—including the children in the pews. Children who encounter God feel the same desire to respond to the living God. Theirs too is the cry of confession, thanksgiving, lament, and adoration. When Christians bar children from the worshiping community

---

8. Charles Wesley, "And Can It Be," in *The Covenant Hymnal*, #306.

or belittle their concerns as too small or trivial, they cut off the young's need to respond to the work of God in their own lives, truncating their conversation with God. Not only does cutting off children's dialogue with God counteract Christ's words to "Let the little children come to me, and do not stop them" (Matt 19:14), but it also negatively affects the entire congregation. When children are not present in the worshiping life of the church, congregations miss out on the unique way children experience and respond to God that can greatly enrich the entire congregation's worship and understanding of God. Perhaps many worship services miss the central components of awe, mystery, and wonder that should be part and parcel of the Christian life because children—those people uniquely suited to see the awesome, mysterious, and wonderful—are missing from the larger worshiping community. We will return to this theme in chapter 5.

Worship Is Enacted

Building off the God-centered and dialogical aspects of worship, worship is also enacted. This proposition first suggests that, as John Burkhardt notes, worship "is something to be *done*."[9] Liturgical scholar Aidan Kavanagh indicates that Christians learn who they are in relation to God by participation. "Prayer cannot be taught; it can only be learned by being around people who pray much and well."[10] If worship is the primary boundary defining our relationship to God, as Bruckner and others suggest, then worship is also the way we practice ourselves into a deeper relationship with God and grow into our nature as created and coworkers with Christ. In short, worship is vocational training, or formation, and a necessary skill of the people of God.

From its inception, Judeo-Christian worship has an embodied physicality that calls on each member of the congregation to an active role in the worship of God. Each Sunday, worshipers come in and find their place in the congregation, perhaps smelling incense or freshly baked bread within the sanctuary. They hear words read from the Bible, proclaimed by the pastor. Worshiping voices sing songs and psalms. Bodies move around, embrace in the passing of the peace, and taste the grace in the bread and the cup. Worshipers see the images of the cross, table, and font, representing the very cornerstones of the faith. Worship requires movement. It is active,

9. Burkhardt, *Worship*, 73.
10. Kavanagh, "Teaching through the Liturgy," 45.

kinesthetic, and embodied, and it requires congregational participation if it is to truly be "the work of the people"—as liturgy is most basically defined.[11] Burkhardt continues, "Worship like work and play, is basically something to be done, not merely talked about ... For embodied creatures, reality lives, it works and plays, in enactment."[12]

Unfortunately, worship in many church models has become something that is more heard or seen than done. The locus of worship is up front, often on a stage. In this model, the active participants are on the stage and the congregation is the audience who watches the action, who may see and hear a well-performed act, but who rarely participate in the drama itself. In *Purity of Heart Is to Will One Thing*, Søren Kierkegaard notes that understanding the congregation as audience and the preacher or worship leader as performer has much more in common with the theater than with church. He argues that we need to understand all people as performers and God as the audience.[13] While we would tweak Kierkegaard's metaphor to understand God as both audience *and* performer, his metaphor underscores the need for active participation on the part of the entire congregation.[14] Worship is not passive or something that happens *to* us; it is something in which we actively engage.

Why is enactment so important? Christian theologians emphasize the importance of worship and liturgy in shaping Christian character and identity. John Westerhoff calls worship the most important factor that shapes faith, character, and consciousness.[15] The late worship professor Robert Webber's *Worship Is a Verb* proclaims, "Worship celebrates Christ; it is God who is speaking and acting; we respond to God and to each other; all creation joins in worship."[16] Robert Browning and Roy Reed call worship the way we learn to be Christian.[17] By practicing worship as a whole congregation, we enact, and hence strengthen, an identity.

11. This is seen in the roots of *leitourgia*: *laos* (people) and *ergon* (work). This is the definition given by Wilson-Kastner, *Sacred Drama*, 7.

12. Burkhardt, *Worship*, 73.

13. Kierkegaard, *Purity of Heart*, 180–81.

14. This is similar to the critique of Kierkegaard's metaphor made by Brink, "Who's the Host," 2.

15. Anderson, "Liturgical Catechesis," 352.

16. Webber, *Worship Is a Verb*, 88.

17. Anderson, "Liturgical Catechesis," 352.

Worship Is Storied

Claiming that worship is enactment begs the question, what is worship enacting? If worship is to be Christian worship, it must be *storied*, and not just by any story, but by the all-encompassing dramatic story of the triune God. This story was begun by God through creation, will end with God in the eschaton, and is centered on the work of God in the life, death, and resurrection of Jesus Christ through the power of the Holy Spirit. As Sara Maitland describes,

> It begins at the beginning (if not before), goes on to the end and then does not stop. There is a Grand Narrative. It is the creative, redemptive and eschatological narrative, centered on the passion, death and resurrection, and developed outwards in all possible directions. It is the workings of God in and with the whole cosmos, and it can be spoken, at least a little, because it has revealed its formal structure in the Word—the creative word and the redemptive word, which (who) is Jesus Christ.[18]

When we come to worship, we come to enact *this* particular story about *this* particular God in all of its brilliance and mystery, depth and simplicity, suffering and celebration. Perhaps no one sums this up more succinctly than Robert Webber in his classic work *Ancient-Future Worship* when he makes the simple yet profound claim, "Worship does God's story."[19]

Children naturally inhabit the world of story. How many times has a small grove of trees been turned into a magical forest and a discarded stick into a wand by a child who has an abundance of time and wonder? Whether children walk through a wardrobe into an enchanted land with C. S. Lewis' Pevensie children, fight off dementors and search for horcruxes with J. K. Rowling's Harry, Ron, and Hermione, or travel with Madeleine L'Engle's Mrs Whatsit, Mrs Who, and Mrs Which by means of tesseracts, children desire to be part of a story that is larger than themselves. They, like us, are looking for stories that carry within them explanations of life. After all, is this not what we all desire in some way? A story that is bigger than ourselves, a life with meaning, a narrative arc giving grace for our past, strength for our present, and hope for our future? If children can be so readily drawn into these fictional stories, how much more should they be

18. Maitland, *A Big-Enough God*, 115.
19. Webber, *Ancient-Future Worship*, 29.

drawn into the living, moving, and breathing story of God—one that asks them not only to listen or imagine but to inhabit and live.

Richard Middleton and Brian Walsh underscore the difference of the biblical story in their book *Truth Is Stranger Than It Used to Be,* when they relate a scene from the popular fantasy movie *The NeverEnding Story.* In this scene, the main character, Bastian, a young boy and bibliophile, finds refuge in an old, run-down bookstore where he has escaped bullies intent on throwing him into a dumpster. As he is searching the shelves, he sees a particularly old and beat-up book that catches his interest. Middleton and Walsh pick up the scene here:

> "What is that book about?" asks Bastian.
>
> "Oh, this is something *special,*" says the bookstore owner.
>
> "Well, what is it?
>
> "Look, your books are safe," the owner says. "By reading them you get to be Tarzan, or Robinson Crusoe."
>
> "But that's what I like about them," replies Bastian.
>
> "Ah, but afterwards you get to be a little boy again."
>
> "What do you mean?" asks Bastian.
>
> "Listen," says the man. "Have you ever been Captain Nemo, trapped inside your submarine while the giant squid is attacking you?"
>
> "Yes," says Bastian.
>
> "Weren't you afraid you couldn't escape?"
>
> "But it's only a *story*!"
>
> "That's what I'm talking about," says the man, "the ones *you* read are safe."
>
> "And this one isn't?"[20]

Of course, this curiosity is too much for Bastian, and he ends up stealing the book. What he finds different about this book is that it does not remain confined to his imagination, but instead he is transported to the actual world of the book. He embarks on an adventure that calls him to make difficult choices and face both great triumph and tragedy along the way.

The adventure of God's salvation story, including triumphs and tragedy, the exciting and the mundane, defines what it means for the faithful to be transported into the actual world of the Christian story. While people may initially come to church to experience a nice morning seeing neighbors, singing pleasant music, hearing messages on morality, and then enjoying a cup of coffee and a donut on the way out, this will never fulfill

20. *The NeverEnding Story,* 1984.

the great longing and vocation of the Christian. Believers come to worship to be drawn into the story of God, to find a place in the plot of God's redemptive work in our lives, our relationship, our world. Children do not need another social activity or another place to learn good manners. They need a story that gives them meaning and purpose in a world where competing, lesser stories and allegiances abound. Not only does storied worship captivate children, it draws them into something worth being captivated by—the redemptive and dramatic story of God.

Worship Is Enacted by All

Finally, worship is God's story enacted by the people of God—*all* the people of God. All persons incorporated into the church through baptism have the responsibility and need to enact God's story through worship in order to find their place in that dramatic story and, more importantly, to give praise to the triune God. It is the call of *all* people, from the cooing infant in her crib, to the twenty-three-year-old man with Down syndrome who looks forward to making the short walk from his home every Sunday morning to the local church. Praising God in worship is the call of the Alzheimer's patient who no longer knows family members but who still mouths the words to "Amazing Grace" as it is played on the out-of-tune, upright piano in the corner of her residence's visitor's lounge. Praising God in worship is the call of the CEO reciting the creed next to the janitor who cleans her office, as well as the four-year-old who marvels at how big God's church and God's story truly are. These people of different ages, genders, ethnicities, and walks of life all come together in their great diversity to raise a unified voice of praise to God.

While this is the ideal of worship, more often than not we see the fractioning of worship into subcategories formed around similar age groups, affinities, ethnicities, or classes. Clearly this is a poor representation of the kingdom of God, where the walls that divide us in the world are meant to be broken down through the work of Christ's death and resurrection (Eph 2:13ff.). As well, worshipers are left bereft of the picture of God's story in its fullness without the diversity of worshipers who gather to tell God's story. So when upper-class people gather together to worship God, they may tell the story of God's goodness and faithfulness expressed through thanksgiving; yet doing so in that limited context misses the voices that speak of humanity's great need, of God's miraculous provision, and misses the cries of lament raised by the oppressed at the injustices in the world. A diversity of people is needed in order to tell the multivalent story of God.

It is for these reasons that children are necessary in worship. Children have the same responsibility and need to offer their response of praise to God. If this role is taken away from them, especially if it is substituted with little more than a Christianized daycare, we do a great disservice to the ones who have been made exemplars of the faith by Jesus himself. More to the point, how are we to "become like little children" in the faith if we are always separated from children in worship? When we isolate children from the worshiping community, we miss out on their distinct voices that tell us something unique about God and God's kingdom.

Sacraments: Identity, Formation, and Service

We have addressed questions of worship and why children are important to corporate worship, yet a final question still looms: why focus specifically on worship as the preeminent formative agent for children? Aren't there other means, such as education, family, or technology, that are equally if not better suited to constructing meaning in the lives of children? What about Sunday school, children's church, and vacation Bible schools? These all seem to serve the common purpose of forming children's identity in faith. Why place the worship life of children as the central focus of this book?

First, God has promised to meet us in worship, specifically in the celebration of the sacraments. Jesus tells us in the Gospel of Matthew that "where two or more are gathered in my name, I am there among them" (Matt 18:20). Obviously, this is the case at other times outside of worship (e.g., Bible studies or Sunday school), but weekly Sunday worship is the place *par excellence* where Christians gather in the name of Jesus to worship the triune God. Further, in the sacraments of baptism and the Eucharist, Christ has promised not only to be present among us but to be present in the simple elements of water, wine, and bread. These sacraments are, as St. Augustine famously noted, "visible signs of invisible grace" that not only remind us of the work of God but are an integral part of the work of God in transforming, redeeming, and nourishing the body of Christ for the sake of all creation. It is therefore through our encounters with God in (but not limited to) worship and the sacraments that we are formed and continually reformed into the people of God.

Worship is specifically suited to formation because of its habitual and ritual nature that forms our ethical lives. While a technical study of Christian ritual and ethics goes beyond the scope of this work, a few cursory points are helpful in underscoring the formative power of worship.[21] Most basically, it is those things we do most regularly and to which we give primacy that powerfully shape who we are and who we become. Whether it is running five miles a day, practicing the violin for two hours daily, spending six hours a day in front of the computer or television screen, or drinking three cups of coffee each morning, the actions we repeat and the habits we form make us the people we are. Setting aside Sunday morning as sacred time for the express purpose of worshiping the triune God is a habit that forms us into people aware of God's sovereignty, grateful of God's grace, and assured of God's provision. As we grow more scientifically and psychologically aware of how formative the period of childhood is, we become that much more aware of the importance of children's having an expressed, regular time of worship.[22]

Further, the rituals within the worship service practiced week after week similarly form a child's (and adult's!) understanding of God, themselves, and their place in the universe. To repeat similar words and actions each Sunday is like the river that over thousands of years slowly carves out a canyon through which it flows. Like the formation of the canyon, this process is neither uniform nor devoid of loss, but in the loss there is a brilliance and beauty revealed in the depths of our humanity where the *imago Dei* remains beneath the layers of our pretenses and vices.

To take but one example, a weekly prayer of confession followed by absolution communicates that our lives are not always lived as they should be, that something is indeed broken, but that we serve a gracious God who forgives the sins of all who confess. It communicates to the child that God's grace has the final word, and it is indeed, as the old hymn tells us, "greater

21. For resources regarding the connection between liturgy and ethics, see Searle, "Liturgy and Social Ethics: An Annotated Bibliography" and Laytham and Bjorlin, "Worship and Ethics." In our study the following works (among many others) have been foundational: Saliers, "Liturgy and Ethics: Some New Beginnings"; Hauerwas and Wells, *The Blackwell Companion*, particularly part 1: "Studying Ethics through Worship"; Wilson, "Liturgy and Ethics"; and Wells, *Improvisation*.

22. Yet we agree with the warning sounded by Willimon in *Service of God* when he states, "We do not worship God in order to become better people. Christians worship God simply because we are God's beloved ones. Christian worship is an intrinsic activity. But as we worship, something happens to us" (37). Worship is primarily for the glorification of God that *then* necessarily forms us.

than all our sin." It also encourages within a child the virtue of gracious living, reconciliation with family and friends, and the preeminence of forgiveness. In short, such ritual teaches a child to live graciously with others and
with oneself in the light of God's unmerited and unyielding grace. We will
discuss the specific ethical virtues promoted in worship in greater depth
in chapter 5, but suffice it to say, Christian ritual over time creates within
the worshiper a specifically Christian story to inhabit—a story that frames
our lives and gives us the raw materials from which we view the world,
construct meaning, and make both mundane and momentous decisions.

The importance of habit and ritual in the worshiping life of a child
presents a strong case for certain fixed elements within worship. Our God
is a permanent one, and worship that reflects this truth builds constancy
in the life of the believing community. When churches give in to cultural
pressures of consumerism, they may end up approaching almost chronic
liturgical innovations as normative.[23] Not only is this a quick recipe for
burnout for pastors and worship leaders, it also presents a skewed notion of
God. God continues to do a new thing, but how does constant innovation
in worship reflect the God who is the same yesterday, today, and forever?
Where might we grasp the continuity of God's story and our connection to
the communion of saints who have gone before us? Further, what happens
to the quality of liturgical elements (songs, prayers, sermons) when worship leaders assume that songs and prayers need be routinely discarded so
the congregation does not grow tired of them? Perhaps just as consumerism has negatively affected the quality of our clothing and appliances (since
no one is really going to wear a pair of jeans for more than a year or two,
why make them out of quality, durable materials?), so too has consumerism
negatively affected the quality of our liturgy.

The importance of ritual and constancy lead naturally to a discussion of sacraments as a regular element of worship life. The sacraments are
central to our understanding of worship in general and to children's place
in worship specifically. Throughout the history of the church, sacraments
have been understood as the primary act of the church where, by God's
gracious initiative, the elements are visible symbols of God's invisible grace.
Some argue that the sacraments point to the power of the Word made flesh,
particularly when it comes in response to the sermon. The sacraments not
only serve as the foundational liturgical actions of the church, they provide

23. For a profound treatment of consumerism in the church, especially as it pertains
to children, see chapter 3 in Mercer's *Welcoming the Children*.

a lens through which to interpret all liturgical acts and the Christian life. Moreover, they bind and reinforce the meaning of Christian identity and service to God's church. We now turn to a discussion of each.

Baptism

Two-year-old Kate reached toward the font, her hand hovering over the water. The words "I baptize you in the name of the Father, and of the Son, and of the Holy Spirit" inspired her to make a move for the sacred water. The congregation responded with anticipation, watching this two-year-old who dared to enact the liturgy on her own. Silence made way for sacredness, and that morning, Kate's openness to God's watery grace struck wonder and joy throughout the nave. Her baptism clearly took, or, more accurately, she took her baptism.

Here we develop baptism as the foreground of all Christian worship. Moreover, the church's historical practice of baptism provides the foundation for the liturgical participation of children. Infant baptism grew in part out of the church's emphasis on the significance of the family.[24] The moral category "the church as family" positions ecclesiology as the template for understanding the inner relations of each member of the church-household, including children. Believer baptism emerged in the context of the state church, which equated citizenship with baptism. In an effort to cultivate Christians who claimed faith and discipleship, believer baptist traditions emphasized the importance of new birth as the ground for incorporation into the church. We begin with an overarching theology of baptism and then address the modes of infant and believer traditions, as each has potential to contribute richly to the participation of children in worship.

The rite offers many symbols that help us discern what God is doing to and for us in the waters of baptism. Through baptism, we join in Christ's death and resurrection as we are submerged into the waters (representing death and the tomb) and emerge with the risen Christ (Rom 6:3–4). In the waters of baptism, we, like Christ, are empowered by the Holy Spirit for ministry (Matt 3:16). In baptism, we are clothed with the new garments of Christ that make us all equal in the sight of God (Gal 3:28–29). However, perhaps the most basic baptismal symbol is that of incorporation. When Paul discusses membership in the body of Christ, he begins by arguing that their baptisms first conjoined these disparate members to the church: "For

24. Weil, "Children and Worship," 56.

just as the body is one and has many members, and all the members of the body, though many, are one body, so it is with Christ. For in the one Spirit we were all baptized into one body—Jews or Greeks, slaves or free—and we were all made to drink of one Spirit" (1 Cor 12:12–13). Through the waters of baptism we are united to the body of Christ, the church.

As we are incorporated into the body of Christ, we are also given a new primary identity. One's identity up to that point—teacher, mother, doctor, brother, child, baby—becomes secondary to our primary call as children of God and as members of Christ's church through the power of the Holy Spirit. As the Latin root *vocatio* implies, through our baptisms we are "called" or "summoned" into a new story with a new history and future, a new set of allegiances, and an entirely new vocation. As the Westminster Catechism asserts, this vocation is to "glorify God and enjoy [God] forever." Obviously, such worship and glorification of God is not limited to a worship service. All life is to be lived for the glory of God. However, the public and communal worship of God in the liturgical life of the church is the primary way in which we uniquely embody our Christian identity and vocation. As Vatican II's influential *Sacrosanctum Concilium* (*Constitution on the Sacred Liturgy*) asserts, a "full, conscious and active participation" in the liturgy is a Christian's "right and duty by reason of their baptism."[25] The primary vocation of the Christian called through the waters of baptism is the worship of the triune God.

From this sacramental viewpoint, baptized people (including children preparing for baptism) share a common liturgical vocation based in identity. All who move from or toward baptism have the *right* and *duty* to participate fully, consciously, and actively in the worshiping life of the church, for they are members of the body of Christ. If we truly believe the message of Paul that the "members of the body that seem to be weaker are indispensable, and those members of the body that we think less honorable we clothe with greater honor" (1 Cor 12:22–23), it is incumbent upon the church to offer children an indispensable, honorable position within its life of worship. Embodied, children thus become a part of liturgical leadership on Sunday morning, whether through processing in and/or serving communion, reading Scripture, singing, lighting candles, passing the peace, or leading prayers, to name but a few examples.

In the earliest recordings of the Christian church, children participated in various aspects of the Christian life. North African theologian

25. *Constitution on the Sacred Liturgy*, 14.

Cyprian of Carthage consistently defended paedobaptism. Not wanting to refuse God's grace to any, he wrote that in baptism, God is Father to all.[26] Others, such as Tertullian, argued that it was more advantageous to wait until the child was able to comprehend the meaning of baptism. Augustine was a proponent of infant baptism; however, he did not believe it to be the only way one becomes alive in Christ. Even in cases where infants were not baptized, children of all ages were dedicated into the flock and participated in the worship and prayer life of the church.[27] Such rituals as the infant kiss, salt on the tongue, conferring of Christian names, reading Scripture (even memorizing it for proclamation before the young lector could read!), singing, and blessing by signing the cross were all means by which infants and children were included in the liturgy.

Yet like the eyes and head in Paul's body metaphor in 1 Corinthians 12, too often in the worshiping life of the church we, by word and deed, tell children, "We have no need of you." This message weakens not only the worshiping life of the child, but the life of the entire church. Through the waters of baptism children are incorporated fully into the body of Christ, a body where the least are the greatest, the margins are the center, and the most vulnerable are the most cherished. This countercultural vision must be embodied in the worshiping life of the church for us to reflect the body of Christ to which we have been called through baptism.

In this discussion of baptism, we consider how the modes of infant and believer baptisms fit into the idea that from baptism one receives a new identity, along with a vocation to participate in worship and serve the church. Our denomination, the Evangelical Covenant Church, affirms Christian unity in baptism and practices both paedobaptism and believer baptism. Theologically, both are valid modes of baptism and point to God's grace working in the life of the baptizand (and the community). A theology of baptism that encompasses both modes signifies the mystery and magnitude of God's grace in the world. Infant modes emphasize God's initiation of grace, connect with our identity as children of God, anticipate God's work in the life of the child, and confess the importance of the church's mission in passing on the faith. Believer modes emphasize the person's response to God's initiation of grace, connect with our identity as disciples, anticipate that a person will continue to make daily decisions to follow Jesus Christ, and confess the importance of the church having instilled in the believer a

26. Cyprian quoted in Horn and Martens, *"Let the Little Children Come,"* 280.
27. Ibid., 290.

vocational mission. In the infant mode, the context is one of dependency and mystery. In believer baptism, the context is one of vocation and mission. Both stem from a new identity.

The astute reader will assent to every aspect that each mode emphasizes, connects with, anticipates, and confesses. In fact, we would argue that the two modes together offer a richer theology of baptism than each does on its own. Each emphasis affirms the right things—God's bestowing a new identity, the church's work of formation that happens in worship and extends into daily life, and the sense that all will eventually find their place in the mission of God's church. When both believer and infant baptism are received together, the church may think of its worship, including baptism's regular place in it, as the place where identity takes root and vocation takes form. Baby Kate may not yet articulate her name as "child of God." However, the people in her life believe this is her new name, and with the constancy of worship, she may continue to enact the liturgy again.

Eucharist

On a Sunday morning a woman enters her local church for worship with her two children. As she enters, her mind races with both the quotidian demands of life—bills, shopping lists, workplace conflict—and the larger concerns of her faith—the indissoluble mix of thanksgiving and lament, faith and fear, assuredness and doubt. At the entrance to the sanctuary, she dips her hand into the waters of the octagonal font. As her hand touches the water, she is reminded that in the midst of her worries and fears, she is a baptized child of God called to this place for worship. She takes her place in the midst of the congregation, singing praise to God, confessing sin and receiving words of forgiveness, hearing and responding to the word of God, and finally coming to the table to receive the body and blood of Christ before being sent back out into the ordinariness of her days.

On this Sunday morning, the woman has traveled the basic path of the Christian life between font and table. The journey is liturgical, in that she makes this literal journey in worship, and eschatological, in that she understands the power of grace to infiltrate her daily life. Those who have been called by the waters of baptism to the vocation of worship are uniquely called to the table for strength and sustenance to remain on the journey of faith. Biblical and historical witnesses affirm that the basic liturgical acts at Christian gatherings were the hearing of the word, the breaking of the bread, and sharing of the cup—in short, word and table. The Eucharist serves as both the means and end of worship or, as Vatican II's *Lumen Gentium* (*The Dogmatic Constitution on the Church*) asserts, the "source and summit of Christian life."[28] Since the reforms of Vatican II, almost every denominational tradition has increased both the frequency of the Eucharist and the theological attention given to the rite. In the liturgical life of the church, the Eucharist has been rediscovered as the natural outflow of the Christian life birthed in the waters of baptism.

Eschatologically, the journey between font and table represents the entire movement of the Christian life from birth to final redemption in the coming kingdom of God. The font has long been associated with the womb where people are born again in the kingdom of God. The beautiful inscription on a Roman baptistery makes such connection explicit:

> Here is born in Spirit-soaked fertility
> a brood destined for another City,
> begotten by God's blowing
> and borne upon this torrent
> by the Church their virgin mother.
> Reborn in these depths they reach for heaven's realm,
> the born-but-once unknown by felicity.
> This spring is life that floods the world,
> the wounds of Christ its awesome source,
> Sinner sink beneath this sacred surf
> that swallows age and spits out youth.
> Sinner here scour sin away down to innocence
> for they know no enmity who are by
> one font, one Spirit, one faith made one.
> Sinner, shudder not at sin's kind and number,
> for those born here are holy.[29]

Similarly, the common spherical shape of fonts is an artistic representation of the womb. The font is then understood as the womb from which the Christian is born anew into the kingdom of God.

If the font is the womb of the Christian life, the table is the *telos*. The table not only represents the Paschal mystery of Christ's death and

---

28. *The Dogmatic Constitution of the Church*, 11.

29. The inscription is often attributed to Pope Sixtus III.

resurrection, it also represents the banquet table in the consummated kingdom of God. Communion is the final great banquet (Luke 14:15–24), where "many will come from east and west and will eat with Abraham and Isaac and Jacob in the kingdom of heaven" (Matt 8:11). It is the marriage supper of the Lamb (Rev 19:6–9) where we will gather with the multitude of saints throughout all time and space to feast at Christ's table. Each time we receive communion in our churches, we participate in a foretaste of that heavenly banquet that is our birthright as children of God born of the baptismal waters. Font and table are a symbolic description of the arc of the Christian story from creation to new creation in the eschaton.

If indeed there is an intrinsic connection between the central sacramental acts of the font and the table, it should cause us to reevaluate the role of children in the worshiping community and the formative effect the sacraments play in the life of participants. In paedobaptist traditions, it is essential that those baptized into the one body of Christ be given access to the body and blood of Christ at the table, for it is at the table that they fulfill their *telos*. At the table they are once again re-membered to the body of Christ. At the table, they are given "food for the journey to which God has called us."[30] Often those who discourage the communion of children point out that children cannot understand the true nature of the Eucharist. However, if we must first cognitively understand the Eucharist before partaking, then none of us should partake, because none of us can truly explain the mystery (the word most related to sacrament in the bible is the Greek *mysterion*) of the sacraments. As liturgical scholar James White reminds us, sacraments—both baptism and the Eucharist—are primarily God's gracious self-giving to the people of God.[31] We do not make the sacraments efficacious by our own cognitive understanding or even by our piety, but we participate in the gracious gift of God's presence made known in the water, bread, and wine. Children and adults called through the waters of baptism must participate in communion in the "now" so that we receive the grace and strength to strive for that which we are "not yet," until the present and coming kingdom of God is fully realized on earth as it is in heaven.

If children and young adults are given access to the table, the rite itself reasserts the importance of the full participation of these groups in all other aspects of the church's liturgical life. At the table, we who eat of the body and blood are reconstituted into the body of Christ and drawn together in

30. "Holy Communion III," in *The Covenant Book of Worship*, 177.

31. White, *Sacraments as God's Self-Giving*.

sacred communion with one another. Before the Apostle Paul bases the united body in our common baptism in 1 Corinthians 12, he first connects the united body to the Eucharist in 1 Corinthians 10: "Because there is one bread, we who are many are one body, for we all partake of the one bread" (10:17). This is the explicit meaning of the term "communion," which comes from the Latin *communio*, literally meaning "mutual participation." Through the mutual participation of the Paschal mystery in the Eucharist, we are drawn into community and mutual participation within the body of Christ—the church. Just as our common baptism draws us into the body of Christ where the least are given the greatest respect, so too the sharing of the common loaf and cup reincorporates us into that same Body and reinforces the necessity of a shared liturgical life for all who partake.

For believer baptist traditions (or traditions such as the Evangelical Covenant Church who affirm both infant and believer baptism), children preparing for baptism must be catechized to the sacraments of the church to prepare them to participate in the central liturgical acts of the church. By witnessing these liturgies before they are formally initiated, children receive a framework to help them prepare for their own initiation into the mysteries of Christ.

Conclusion

The world of three-year-old Elijah reflects the worship of the church in a profound way. Likely, the fact that Elijah witnessed and participated in the sacrament of the Eucharist each week created such an impression that Elijah chose to repeat it in play. Hearing the same words of invitation each week enabled him to recall them and repeat them expertly. Perhaps there were occasions when other children witnessed the communion game as well! Through the habit of weekly worship and the rituals that compose the liturgy, children gain a way to see the world. This is not a nihilistic world of meaninglessness and chaos, nor a utopian world where tragedy and pain are ignored, but a beautiful, broken world shot through with the glory and grandeur of God, a world God so loved that God sent Jesus, the Son of God, to bring about redemption by the power of the Holy Spirit—a world waiting to be redeemed with the help of the child.

Children
Worship
Incorporation
Virtue
Vocation
Vision

3. Incorporation

Orthodox theology teaches that the Son alone can be represented in iconography. Yet Andrei Rublev's icon of the Old Testament Holy Trinity (ca. 1422) reveals three divine persons communing around a table. The Father sits on the left, looking to the Son and Spirit. The Holy Spirit sits on the right, looking to the Father. Christ is in the middle, and while he is also looking to the Father, his body is turned toward the Holy Spirit. The beautiful blend of glance and posture is panoptic, in that the three are fully attentive to one another in perfect unity.

Breaking with tradition, Rublev courageously depicted the three persons as one being in perfect unity and love, and the Council of Moscow (1551) commended it as an exemplar for future iconographic art. Orthodox theologian Paul Evdokimov declared its unique place in theological history, writing "In this icon, Rublev recreated the very rhythm of Trinitarian life. He also was able to show its unified diversity and the movement of love that identifies the Persons without confusing them."[1] For the first time in iconography, the three persons of the Godhead were shown in their mutuality and equality.

The all-embracing spirit of the icon is not limited to the immanence of the three persons of the Trinity, for the reader herself is incorporated into the truth that Rublev's work reveals.[2] The posture of the three as well

1. Evdokimov, *The Art of the Icon*, 245.
2. In iconography, the author writes, rather than paints, the icon. Iconography

as the full view of each face invite the reader into the divine communion. In glorious unity, the three welcome the icon reader to the empty place at the table to share the meal. Readers find themselves encompassed in the circle around the table, and it is easy to imagine oneself a recipient of the incorporating activity of Father, Son, and Holy Spirit.

Our primary metaphor describing the church's worship activity is "incorporation," which refers to the economy of love that exists within the Trinity. This love unifies the three while engaging the difference within the divine community. Notions of the oneness of the church, communion in the body, and unity in difference are all ways of describing the economy of love within the people of God. Oneness, communion, and unity require cooperative work and a deep sense of humility in the face of the diversity of persons at God's table.

Other terminology exists, of course. For example, the cooperative efforts of the church point to the desire to be inclusive. Inclusivity connotes hospitality and transcends boundaries. It is a promising goal for the church to work toward; however, dimensions of difference, differentiation, and diversity can get lost in the desire for inclusivity, and one of the goods at stake in this project is the preservation and particularity of difference and differentiation, specifically as it pertains to children.

In his book *The Christian Imagination: Theology and the Origins of Race*, theologian and black church studies professor Willie James Jennings describes an experience of being "included."[3] Jennings was a young boy playing in his yard in Grand Rapids when two white men approached the house with the intent of evangelizing to Jennings' mother. Over the next lengthy bit of time, the men proceeded to fill the space with accolades about their church's ministry, culminating in an invitation for the Jennings family to join them. At the end of the speech, Jennings' mother interrupted, "I am already a Christian. I believe in Jesus." She continued, explaining to the men that she was a very active member of New Hope Missionary Baptist Church, just down the block. The men talked a little more and then left Jennings' mother with some literature. Jennings remembers thinking to himself, "Why did they not know us? They should have known us very well."[4]

originated with the intent to write, through picture, the revealed truths of Scripture in a way that was accessible to the non-literate Christian world. Thus we continue to engage icons as readers rather than viewers today. Inherent in an icon is an invitation for the reader to enter into the life of God and to find one's place in the story.

3. Jennings, *The Christian Imagination*, 3.
4. Ibid.

Jennings' story illustrates the limits of inclusivity. Inclusivity can mean the participation of the whole, but often it does not. Focusing explicitly on inclusivity can also have a minimal and even detrimental effect. On one level, the white men's intent was very likely one of inclusion. They had intended to invite the Jennings family to be a part of God's kingdom and perhaps even their own church family. But that was not the primary message young Jennings received. Instead, Jennings and his mother felt unknown—the men had blindly neglected the Baptist congregation down the street, lacked the ability to listen and ask questions of the Jennings family up-front, and disregarded the possibility that they were already committed Christians!

In short, the white men exhibited what we call exclusive inclusivity, or inclusivity that lacks the important quality of recognizing and supporting the diversity of people and their experiences. By exclusive inclusivity, we refer to terms or assumptions held by one group seeking to fold—or include—another group into itself. Such a perspective works toward the two, or the many, becoming one. In the process, though, the one being grafted in loses its distinctiveness if it does not have shared participation in such aspects as power, narrative, and representation. If diverse members do not share in participation, difference within unity does not occur in ways that reflect the diversity of members. Were Jennings' encounter with hospitality to be written iconographically, one wonders whether Jennings and his mother would have had an equal place at the table or whether they would have been written in to the story at all.

In this chapter we explore the phenomenon of incorporation as it is reflected in two of the church's central doctrines—the Trinity and Christology. The doctrine of the Trinity engages the distinct difference between the three persons of the Godhead while maintaining the claim that God is one utterly undivided essence. The balance of unity in diversity and diversity in unity characterizes who God is and what God does. The unity of the three connotes love so deep and so rich that nothing can break it up or extract it from the whole. God's life of three in one offers theological depth to the church's work of incorporation as the church seeks to love in ways that reflect the life of God.

The doctrine of Christology further deepens the good of unity in difference, in the way that Christ is fully divine and fully human. The relationship between Christ's two natures serves as an analogue for preserving difference within unity. As Jennings' story demonstrates, the church must deal with questions of power and dominant cultures as it works toward diversity in unity. Recent work in Christology and cultural hybridity provide further context for thinking theologically about differentiation within the body.[5] It also offers a lens to examine how power can operate in ways that stifle diversity.

We address the incorporation of children more fully in chapter 5, which deals with children's vocation. That said, this chapter offers some preliminary suggestions on how these doctrines help the church think through the differentiation of children within the unity of the body. Children represent a kind of difference within the body, and, as we argued in chapter 1, they are part of God's life in communion.

Trinity

God is love, and God loves. At stake in the Christian doctrine of the Trinity is the good news that love constitutes the heart of God's nature. Love, then, is not only the "who" of God but the work that God does within the community of the Godhead and extends into the world. It is both the beginning and end of being, and it directs the beginning and end of the worshiping body. Incorporation in worship, then, is broadly about the economy of love among the three persons of the Godhead.

Classic definitions of the Trinity describe God as three persons in one essence. Historian and theologian Justo González writes of his experience studying the historical debates on the Trinity. At times he felt bogged down by the detailed hairsplitting that accompanied some of the early church's discussions on the Trinity. The eye-opening moment occurred when González considered the context within which the church found itself. Specifically, economic greed and unjust practices were commonplace. In the idea that God is three persons in one, utterly undivided unity, Christianity's forebears found an argument for shared life, including shared resources. In other words, within the doctrine of the Trinity, followers of Christ articulated a robust morality of justice and generosity that informed human practices. Realizing this, González developed his appreciation for the detailed conclusions of the three-in-one debates.

One of the key thinkers involved in historical discussions on the Trinity was St. Basil of Caesarea (b. 330 CE). Basil writes that God's communion

5. See Bantum, *Redeeming Mulatto* and Elizondo, *The Galilean Journey*.

is indissoluble, continuous, without variation or void, and indivisible.[6] In stating the nature of God's "communion of essence," Basil emphasizes the unity even as one encounters the distinction of persons. He clarifies that one may discover the distinct persons of God, but because God is one, an encounter with even one of the three draws persons into the unity of God's communion. None of the three persons is ever simply a person separate from the other two. The Son, the Spirit, and the Father are always together. The connecting Spirit is always the Father's spirit and the Son's spirit. The originating Father is always giving himself over to the Spirit and the Son. And the incarnate Son is always the visible manifestation of Father and Spirit. St. Augustine uses the analogy of the Father as lover, the Son as beloved, and the Spirit as the bond of love between them.[7] Lover, beloved, and love underscore the essential unity that is the Trinity.

The unity and oneness of God mark the mutuality that happens between the three persons of the Godhead. Mutuality emphasizes the freedom of the self-giving love that each member pours into one another and then into creation. Mutuality is relationship without hierarchy, with each part giving over the best of themselves to the others. This is Basil's brilliance in describing the Trinity—the oneness of God is best summed up in two words: close relationship.[8] God's inner relationship is so intimate that the connection itself forms the natural, inseparable, oneness of God's being.

Christianity is a monotheistic faith, and Western Christianity is quite comfortable discussing the unity and indivisible nature of God. Yet God's unity fully incorporates each of the three persons, and the other side of the story of unity is the idea of distinct personhood. In theology, two technical terms signify the differentiation and unity of persons in God's life— hypostatic union and perichoresis. Hypostatic union and perichoresis are descriptive of the three-ness of God's identity and activity, and they offer nuance as we apply Trinitarian theology to the idea of incorporation.

Hypostasis and Difference

One of the beauties of the Christian doctrine of the Trinity is the affirmation of difference. Diversity is a divine attribute. Father, Son, and Spirit never collapse into one. Rather, diversity within the Godhead is maintained

6. St. Basil, *Letters*, 38.4.

7. For more on this see Augustine, *On the Trinity*.

8. St. Basil, *Letters*, 38.5.

both in terms of distinct personhood and in terms of the activity of differentiation. God is three—Father, Son, and Holy Spirit.

The hypostases of God are the particularity of God. Hypostasis is a Greek category meaning "person," and when the early church sought to articulate orthodox ways to talk about who God is and what God does, they settled on the description of three persons—or hypostases—who mutually indwell one being. The perfect union of the three is called the hypostatic union, or the union of the three persons of God.

Basil describes the essence (or unity) as the general and the hypostases (or persons) as the particular.[9] The individual persons give humans a sense of the properties and character of God. Through the three hypostases, we "form our conception of God from the general idea of existence."[10] In describing hypostasis, Basil steers away from numbers and mathematics to focus instead on the richness that is each of the hypostases, including the excellence of the particular character of each. He concedes, "Count if you must; but you must not by counting do damage to the faith."[11] Distinguish between the three, while abiding by the one.

Of this unity in difference Basil also writes, "But the communion and the distinction apprehended in Them are, in a certain sense, ineffable and inconceivable, the continuity of nature being never rent asunder by the distinction of the hypostases [or persons], nor the notes of proper distinction confounded in the community of essence."[12] The analogy of a musical piece works well here. The unity of the piece of music points to God's one essence, while the particular notes mark the distinction, even differentiation, of Father, Son, and Spirit. (The strength of this analogy is one reason to assert that a congregation singing is the closest thing to the Trinity this side of eternity!)

In dialogue with patristic sources, Reformed theologian Kathryn Tanner expands the description of hypostasis within the Godhead. The relationship between each of the persons of God clarifies God's oneness and unity. As the Father begets the Son in human form, the Son as Word perfectly images, or refers to, the Father. The Son gives the Spirit form and shape, just as the Spirit prepares the way for the incarnation of the Son. The Spirit is the power of the Father, uniting them in love, and the Father

9. St. Basil, *Letters* 236.6 and 38.2.

10. Ibid., 236.6

11. St. Basil, *De Spiritu Sancto*, 18.44.

12. Ibid., 38.4.

sends the Spirit for mission.[13] This wonderfully intricate set of relationships within the Godhead articulates the distinction of the three persons, who in themselves do not have meaning without the power and connection between them.

The distinctiveness of the three persons and the differentiation within the Godhead serve as the form through which each of the persons—Father, Son, and Holy Spirit—come to know themselves in the presence of the other. The Trinity is an example of knowing oneself through the other, and the perfect mutuality of the three is predicated on hypostatic unity.

The notion of personhood is a human one. Yet when we consider its origin in the Godhead, personhood opens up into a way of being in and through another. It allows individuation and differentiation to be seen as *through* others instead of over and against others. The relationships that happen between persons define the unity and infuse the identity of each and the whole. Most important, the "community of essence," as Basil notes, provides a way for a secure, safe, mutually beneficial understanding of personhood. Incorporation, as another way of describing what we mean by the differentiation of hypostases, offers a model for moving beyond the exclusive inclusivity that Willie Jennings critiques in favor of differentiating activity that gives meaning and substance to the unity of the whole.

Perichoresis and Unity

> The words that I say to you I do not speak on my own; but the Father who dwells in me does his works. Believe me that I am in the Father and the Father is in me; but if you do not, then believe me because of the works themselves. (John 14:10–11)

Jesus' words to Philip in the Gospel of John bespeak the theological notion of perichoresis or the shared activity of the Godhead. Perichoresis is the inner mutuality and power between the three persons. The Greek word *chorein* means to "make room" or "go forward," and *peri* signifies reciprocity.[14] Succinctly, perichoresis is "the dynamic process of making room for another around oneself."[15] The Godhead's activity is defined by the three persons moving in and through each other. Father Robert Kress writes,

13. Tanner, *Christ the Key*, 185–93.
14. Lampe, *A Patristic Greek Lexicon*, 1077.
15. M. G. Lawler quoted in Manastireanu, *A Perichoretic Model of the Church*, 77.

"The term describes the intensely intimate presence of the Father, Son, and Holy Spirit with, to, and in one another."[16] The profound simplicity of his description reveals presence as characteristic of perichoresis in God's life.

While hypostasis refers to identity and the distinction of persons, perichoresis includes the shared *activity* and *power* that comes from the persons "making room" for one another. Some theologians describe perichoresis as the dance of the Godhead, whereby the whole Trinity shares in the movement of each person. Another portrayal is to say each member brings glory to the whole. John's Gospel, for example, offers numerous descriptions of how Father, Son, and Holy Spirit glorify one another in all they do.

In perichoretic imagery, the unity of the Trinity emerges from its dynamic, shared work. German theologian Jürgen Moltmann writes that the activity of the Trinity is "open, inviting unity, capable of interaction."[17] God's activity grounds the unity, rather than serving as some kind of derivative of the unity. Another way to describe the dynamic activity of the Trinity is in terms of circulation and the exchange of love that targets each of the others, while also drawing creation into the common life of the Godhead. This is a description of the *missio dei* in broad terms.

While some of the earlier church fathers attend to perichoresis in their work, St. John of Damascus offers a robust summary of its theological development. He uses images of boundless power, fountain of goodness and justice, creator of all, maintainer, and preserver to describe the shared activity and power of the three. God is "united without confusion and divided without separation." As the three emerge from mutual essence, they dwell in each other, share will, energy, power, authority, and movement. He helpfully writes of the three's "movement by one impulse."[18] In other words, the activity of one of the persons, such as the incarnation of the Son, makes visible not only the Son but also the Father and Spirit. Differentiation of persons and properties, hence, operate within the Trinity. When compared with human understandings, we note that the differentiation of the Trinity is communicable in properties that are reciprocal and allow the others to be visible, as Rublev seemed to take into account in his icon.

Through language such as encompassing and coinherence, one understands the shared of identity of the Godhead. Yet the language of making

16. Kress, "Unity in Diversity and Diversity in Unity," 67.

17. Moltmann, *The Trinity and the Kingdom*, 149–50.

18. John of Damascus, *An Exposition*, I.8.

room for another, interchange, and reciprocation refer to the activity of incorporation within the Godhead. In other words, participation is a divine method for maintaining unity while preserving difference. The idea of participation is deeply linked with incorporation in that each participates in the other in a way that they become one, while preserving the properties and characteristics of each.[19] A simpler way to put it: the activity of love makes no difference if there is not an other to receive and return love. If that other is subsumed, the exchange of love loses its currency. In continuous circulation, however, love is a divine force that secures unity within difference.

Communion in Difference

Hypostasis and perichoresis are technical yet helpful ways of describing the Trinity because they draw humanity into the truth about the communion of God. Each of the three finds its distinctness through the others. It is not a one-way street in which the Father, for example, defines the Son and the Spirit. Rather, it is a mutual zone within which each becomes itself through another. Episcopal theologian Mark MacIntosh contrasts the difference, arguing that the persons of the Trinity find their identity in the others: "On the one hand, it might mean a self-contained, self-sufficient ego with no need of anybody else; on the other, it can mean someone whose identity is tied up with relationships."[20] MacIntosh goes so far as to say that the Christian's identity mirrors that of God's personhoods in that we strive to become persons through our relationships with others.

In his short story "It Wasn't Me," Wendell Berry returns to his fictional setting of rural Port William, Kentucky, to tell the story of Elton Penn. Elton is the quintessential rugged individualist who strives through hard work and discipline never to be in debt to anyone. For many years, Elton and his wife, Mary, have farmed as tenants on the farm of Old Jack. Anticipating his own death, Old Jack assesses the price of the farm at $200 an acre and wills to the Penns half the value of the farm. Elton, however, bristles at the thought of this free gift. As Wheeler Catlett, a lawyer, neighbor, and friend of Elton, describes him, "Nothing in his experience had prepared him for a benefit that was unasked, unearned, and unexpected. Nothing

19. For more on this, see Otto, "The Use and Abuse of *Perichoresis* in Recent Theology," 366–84.

20. MacIntosh, *Mysteries of Faith*, 35.

in his character prepared him to be comfortable with an obligation that he could not pay."[21] To complicate matters further, Old Jack's daughter decides to go against her father's wishes and auction off the land to the highest bidder, thereby guaranteeing that the price will go above $200 an acre. Yet Elton finally is talked into going to the auction and readies himself to go as high as $235. When the bidding starts, it quickly escalates beyond his means, and he and Mary prepare to leave empty-handed. Unwilling to see it end this way, Wheeler works his way through the crowd behind Elton, grabs him by the arm, and encourages him, "Go on! ... It'll be alright! Go on." Emboldened by the support, Elton takes the bid at $300 an acre.

After the elation of the win wears off, Elton fears he has made a huge financial mistake. Elton goes to Wheeler's office and reveals his fears of losing the farm. Wheeler replies firmly, "No, my boy. You're not going to lose it. Not if we *both* can help it. I told you to go ahead because it would be alright. You must understand that I meant that. If you need help, I'm going to help you." Elton continues to protest and finally reaches the crux of the matter, when he blurts out, "I want to make it on my own. I don't want a soul to thank." Elton understands that he is now indebted twice over: first to Old Jack and now to Wheeler. In his wisdom, Wheeler replies, "Well, putting aside whatever Mary Penn might have to say about that, and putting aside what it means in the first place to be a living human, I don't think your old friend (Old Jack) has left you in a shape to be thankless ...[Y]ou're indebted to a dead man. So am I. So was he. That's the story of it ... It's no use to want to make it on your own, because you can't."[22]

Elton learns that part of what it means to be human is to be dependent on one another, to be caught up in the stories of those who have gone before us, those who are our neighbors, and those who will come after us. The story of Elton Penn indeed always includes the story of Mary Penn and Wheeler Catlett and Jack Beecham and all the people whose lives have formed the web of community in the small town of Port William. It is finding our humanness in a web of relationships—in love given and received, handed over and down, poured out and cupped into our meager and shaking hands to be given away again. This community is one in the giving and receiving of love from its many members, in this perichoretic movement.

The implication is that one's personhood also influences the distinctions of another's personhood. This idea of distinct persons and mutual

21. Berry, "It Wasn't Me," 272.
22. Ibid., 283–84.

influence undergirds the unity in difference that marks the body of Christ and offers a lens for understanding the incorporation of children as distinct human beings. If we take the trinitarian understanding of persons through hypostasis and perichoresis rather than human definitions of the person as a separate and isolated body and soul, then the Godhead becomes a defining aspect of what it means to be a person—always coming into being through relationship and shared activity.

In sum, incorporation describes the very nature of God's triune self as well as God's triune activity. God is one—Father, Son, and Holy Spirit—differentiated yet utterly undivided. The church's shared work is to move and be drawn more deeply into the communal life of the triune God, even while we remain differentiated or fully creaturely. We describe this movement broadly as incorporation—the movement toward union that includes differentiation.

Christology

The ability to incorporate one another in the body of Christ comes from God's extension of grace through Christ. Humans have knowledge of God's life in communion because God has revealed this to humanity in the incarnation of Jesus Christ. The Word made flesh extends the substance of who God is as well as the capacity to become Christ-like. Within the doctrine of Christology, a number of theological claims support the use of incorporation, particularly in its salvific dimensions.

One Hypostasis

The Council of Chalcedon (451) proclaimed that Christ is fully human and fully divine. The claim that Christ is fully divine affirms God's revelation of himself in the person of Jesus Christ. If Christ were not divine, then the revelation is not God himself, and Jesus is mere messenger or teacher. The full divinity of Jesus designates him as member of the Trinity and hence part of the communion of the Godhead. Jesus' divinity is the grounds for humanity's direct access to God.

St. Cyril's work *On the Unity of Christ* points to the unity of the two natures in a profound way. He emphasizes that the two natures of Christ exist together without impeding, stifling, or negating the other, and he argues that similarly, humanity's own union with God also does not impede, stifle, or negate individuality. On the contrary, God's union with humanity in the Incarnation actually frees humanity precisely to flourish and to differentiate in ways that fulfill, rather than subsume, human nature.

The notion of unity in difference is underscored in Cyril's exposition on the anointing of Christ. He argues that all of the divine perfections are common to Father, Son, and Holy Spirit and that all share equal glories— unified as triune God. However, the signification of Christ as "anointed one" denotes the self-emptying of Jesus and Paul's word that Christ was sanctified with us when be became human. The implication is that God's taking on the fullness of humanity means that God made human limitations his own. As human, he is anointed, even while as specifically God he is not. Cyril writes,

> Nonetheless he made the limits of the manhood his own, and all the things that pertain to it, and for this reason he is called Christ even though he cannot be thought of as anointed when we consider him specifically as God or when we speak about his divine nature. How else could we consider that there is one Christ, One Son and Lord, if the Only Begotten had disdained the anointing and had never come under the limitations of the self-emptying? [23]

In Cyril's description of the two natures as they relate to anointing, the differentiation within the unity of God is clear.

Cyril deepened the view of Christ's personhood as it relates to an identity emerging from the kingdom of God. In his introduction to Cyril's *On the Unity of Christ,* patristic scholar John McGuckin discusses the ways in which Cyril resisted defining personhood in terms of the thinking act and instead saw it as transcendent mystery connected with the age of the kingdom.[24] In other words, Christ's identity and subjectivity as a (divine-human) person was God-given as opposed to a kind of psychological subjectivity. An iconic image offers further understanding. Icons of Christ Pantocrator are some of the oldest and date to the sixth century. In these icons, Christ is depicted with two expressions that could be interpreted as representing the two natures of Christ. Even so, the icons depict only one face in the one person, and in this way, the idea of the one person (hypostasis) is also represented.

The unity of the triune God is so strong that it is able to take on radical difference without losing singularity of being. Mark MacIntosh writes that

23. Cyril, *On the Unity of Christ,* 67.
24. Ibid., 41.

"within the unity of divine loving, God has embraced not only what is *other* than God (the creature) but even that which is *antagonistic* to God (the sinner)."[25] God assuming or incorporating that which is other than God is most true in the Incarnation of Jesus Christ. The divine and human nature of Jesus, then, propels us further into the church's work of incorporation as communion in difference.

Two Natures

The actual *relationship* between the divine and human natures of Christ offers yet another level of God's work of incorporation. The question of how the two natures are related has been much debated. The Chalcedonian definition concluded that Jesus Christ is one person with two natures, and these two natures remain intact, not intermingled, separate yet joined in the one person, or hypostasis, of Christ.

Once again, God has revealed himself as a being who bears distinctions within unity. Christologically speaking, the divine nature is fully incorporated into the triune God, while the human nature fully identifies with humanity. The claim that the two natures of Christ are mixed or blurred falls into the error of collapsing differentiation into unity. Cyril writes:

> [T]he flesh, by the principle of its own nature, is different from the Word of God, and conversely the nature of the Word is essentially different from the flesh. Yet even though the elements just named are conceived of as different and separated into a dissimilarity of natures, Christ is nevertheless conceived of as one from both, the divinity and humanity having come together in a true union.[26]

The unity lies in the *personhood* (hypostasis) as opposed to the natures of Christ.

Christological unity is a central claim to salvation because it addresses Christ's unity with God and with humanity. The claim that Christ is human affirms God's complete identification with creation, and most especially human beings. Moreover, it affirms that God overcame the brokenness of human beings' relationship with God by becoming one of them. One of the heresies of the early church was that Jesus was fully God, but only partially

25. MacIntosh, *Mysteries of Faith*, 42.
26. Cyril, *Against Nestorius*, II.33.

human, in that his mind was not human. In disagreement with this idea's proponent, Apollinaris, Gregory of Nazianzus wrote,

> If anyone has put his trust in Him as a Man without a human mind, he is really bereft of mind, and quite unworthy of salvation. For that which He has not assumed He has not healed; but that which is united to His Godhead is also saved. If only half Adam fell, then that which Christ assumes and saves may be half also; but if the whole of his nature fell, it must be united to the whole nature of Him that was begotten, and so be saved as a whole.[27]

Gregory's point is that God's healing is so holistic that the fullness of the human experience is incorporated into God's very being through the Incarnation.

Paul's Letter to the Philippians discusses the Incarnation in kenotic terms that reveal how Christ divested himself of power. He emptied himself, took the form of a slave, and was born in human likeness. The idea of power is turned on its head in the divine willingness to take on human limitations for the sake of uniting humanity with God. In the union of Christ's divinity and humanity, we see the perfect overcoming of brokenness in a complete identification. In other words, Christ's full divinity and humanity link God's outpouring of love and grace, whereby God through Christ incorporates humanity into the divine life.

The contribution that the two natures of Christ offers our understanding of incorporation is tethered to the salvific work of God. Eastern theologians refer to this process in which the divine assumes the human without negating human nature as deification. Deification is most commonly known by Western Christians through Irenaeus' claim that God became what we are (human) so that we could become what God is (divine). This process is rooted in baptism but does not end there, for Irenaeus discusses "making progress day by day," including recovering from sin, ascending toward the perfect, and approximating Christ.[28] In short, difference is incorporated into the divine life in a way that preserves its nature, even while its nature differentiates.

Kathryn Tanner spells out how God becoming human reveals not only the incorporating work within the Trinity but also Christ's incorporation of us.[29] She uses the theological category of imaging to argue that Christ's

27. Gregory Nazianzen, *Letters*, Division I, Ep. CI.

28. Irenaeus of Lyons, *Against Heresies*, Book IV.38.3.

29. Tanner, *Christ the Key*.

humanity perfectly images the divine because both natures are inherent in the Word who is made flesh. The imaging of the divine through the (perfect, sinless, unbroken) human is the paradigm for what it means for human beings to image God. While our capacity to image is imperfect, we are incorporated into that which we are *not* (God) because God's own divinity has incorporated God's humanity. Moreover, Tanner argues that God gives the gift of grace in Jesus Christ not primarily in response to sin but because the possibility for life in Christ—being humans who strongly image their maker—is what God created them for! In short, human "nature" is made for attachment to Christ and incorporation into God's communion. Christ is the possibility for this shared life even while we remain wholly human—diverse yet unified.

Incorporating Children in the Church

These analyses of the Trinity and Christology offer rich insights into what we mean by incorporation as it relates to God's life in communion and God's love for humanity. So what about incorporation on a human level? What do hypostatic unions and perichoretic activity have to do with the church and worship?

Systematic theologian Thomas Torrance argues that perichoresis is deeply connected with the worship life of the church. He writes, "It must be said, therefore, that the basic conception of perichoresis arises out of joyful belief in Jesus Christ as Lord and Saviour, and out of worship and thanksgiving for the saving Love of God as Father, Son, and Holy Spirit who reconciles us to himself and takes us up into Communion with himself."[30] The love within the Trinity points to God's desires for communion with human beings as well as within the Godhead, and herein lies the power for God's incorporating activity to infuse the life of the church.

Miroslav Volf conjoins God's activity and the church's with some depth in an article on generosity in the triune life. He asserts that the joy and delight that is part of God's life rests on the continuous exchange of love for the benefit of the others. He refers to Paul's understanding of spiritual gifts as the way the body of Christ mirrors love's economy, and members offer, by way of exchange, their gifts in effort to nourish a community of love. He writes:

30. Torrance, *Christian Doctrine of God*, 172.

> Unlike simple conjunction, communion presupposes a certain
> degree of like-ness. There is an *affinity* between human beings and
> God, and therefore, between the way Christians—and by exten-
> sion human beings—ought to live and the way God is. The nature
> of God, therefore, fundamentally determines the character of the
> Christian life.[31]

The love within the Godhead communicates the substance of human affinity with God and serves as the model and power for human relationships
with one another. God's tri-unity is one of reciprocity, mutuality, relationship, shared life, communion, and glorifying the other. These characteristics
shape the qualities for which the people of God likewise strive. While these
images of incorporation in the Godhead offer multiple points of ingress
for applying incorporation to the church, the themes of power and presence in the life of God merit additional reflection as they apply to children's
differentiation.

Power

Incorporating difference while maintaining the unity of the body has posed
an almost insurmountable hurdle throughout the church's history. Power is
a key reason for the difficulties of incorporating diversity. Sometimes power
operates directly, but other times its grasp is more subtle. For example, both
of the authors are familiar with churches that are predominantly white, and
while they are urban and exist in multicultural and diverse economic contexts, they generally reflects a white middle-class, educated, liberal culture.
Each congregation has intentionally sought to be welcoming and inclusive
and has to some degree succeeded. Certainly, the doors are "open" to anyone who wishes to enter. Yet, the dominant culture remains constant even
as it invites in those who look or live differently. Why?

The dominant culture itself is bigger and more powerful than the individual or smaller subcultures of any given group. The dominant culture is
largely unable to change because inclusivity and hospitality occur based on
that culture's initiative and terms. Power, narrative, and representation still
occur in what we call the default—or status quo—mode, and any differentiation that might happen within this community does not affect the larger
culture in significant ways. Evangelism professor Soong-Chan Rah writes,
"When a majority culture is dominant, it is that culture that determines

31. Volf, "Being as God Is," 4.

how power is used or distributed."[32] In order to move beyond a monolithic culture to a diverse culture that exhibits unity while incorporating difference, a community needs to divest itself of power. Divestiture requires opening doors to things that make a comfortable group uncomfortable.

This rarely happens by express intention—more frequently, power shifting happens in crises or through changes beyond a dominant group's control. A healthy culture is one that grows in ways that allow other cultures to participate and to shape the work of the group in ways that reflect the particularity that they bring. In an interview on faith and leadership, Rah aptly says, "Unless you're here, the way God made you, my life as a Christian is incomplete. By you being here, bringing your different culture and style of worship and approach to fellowship, my life becomes complete in Christ, because I'm seeing Christ in you the way I can't see Christ just in my own life."[33] His statement resists the kind of exclusive inclusivity that covers up difference.

Social scientists have long recognized the tensions that exist within individuals' desires to individuate and their desires to assimilate as they intersect with culture and power.[34] The importance of differentiation as part of human flourishing has rich support in the African concept of Ubuntu, which describes a sense of self-differentiation that occurs within and with the support of a unified community. Analogous to the idea of inclusion without differentiation discussed earlier in the chapter, emotional fusion is the phenomenon of unhealthy community or togetherness that results in the merging of the self with others. The emotionally fused individual, in other words, is undifferentiated and his/her relations with others, including awareness of both self and others, is diminished.[35]

Emotional fusion can be potentially mistaken as unity within a group or as mutual dependency. In fused communities, individuals and subcultures are overlooked, or "no-selves." One obvious result is a truncated capacity to mature as a community and as individuals. Psychologists use the term self-in-relationship. As we apply the concept to the body of Christ, we further ground the phenomenon and the human capacity to differentiate while remaining together as Christians seek, by God's grace, to emulate the unity in difference within the Trinity.

32. Rah, *Many Colors*, 121.
33. Rah, "Freeing the Captive Church."
34. Majerus and Sandage, "Differentiation of Self," 42.
35. Ibid.

In his book *Redeeming Mulatto*, theologian Brian Bantum addresses identity as it is shaped through responding to difference. He specifically takes up the question of cultural and religious hybridity through the lens of the two natures of Christ.[36] Bantum refers to the Chalcedonian definition, and demonstrates how it resonates with the mulatto/a experience of mixed identity. Using a category that he calls the "mulattic character," he characterizes the complexity of Christ's person as it speaks to those who are of mixed race.

Christ's body, argues Bantum, is both problem and solution. As he examines the church's theological history through themes of purity and racial identity, he finds that it is bound with God's call to incorporate strangers, aliens, and those who are different. The limitations that emerge from God's people are, not surprisingly, related to misuses of power. In particular, the power of identity becomes the location of abuse and oppression within Christianity as it relates and responds to difference. In trinitarian differentiation, as discussed above, identity or personhood emerges in and through the other. Identity comes into being through a mutual and generous self-giving. In human history, identity likewise emerges through an encounter with difference. However, instead of finding oneself in and through another in reciprocal ways, racial identity has emerged as over and against another (different) race. Bantum argues that a primary cause of using power over and against another is the threat of the disruption of self and the lack of presence to an other.

In this social and Christian framework, the hybridity of the mulatto/a is also at once a problem and a solution. It is a problem because of the seeming impossibility that is the mixed race person. Mixed bodies represent the drama of Western identity and identification, and in the end, "the mulatto/as die upon the altar of racial assertion" and reveal "the challenge of racial discipleship." Inversely, this challenge also reveals the possibility for a "wider interpretive matrix of identity or personhood."[37] In other words, the Christian tradition has theological tools and categories at its disposal, rendering it able to find Christ more deeply in our midst by expanding notions of identity and personhood beyond the confines of human brokenness and even subtle misuses of power.

36. Bantum, *Redeeming Mulatto*. For more on recent work in hybridity in theological studies, see Elizondo, "Jesus the Galilean Jew"; Considine, "Is the Future Mestizo and Mulatto?"; Bañuelas, ed., *Mestizo Christianity*.

37. Bantum, *Redeeming Mulatto*, 82.

Bantum's aim is to move beyond modern tendencies of disembodied ideas, on the one hand, and idealizing particular bodies, on the other.[38] This intent is useful in the arena of children and the related tendencies to understand them through the lenses of universal developmental theory and categories of the adult world, on the one hand, or as idealized sites of reception and formation—even Christian formation—on the other. While both tendencies have something to offer the church, taken alone and without adult receptivity to that which is *not* adult, namely the child, the gift and creativity that God has made in the child is muted or lost.

The divesting of power that humans witness in Christ's self-limitation models the ways that adults might limit themselves in the interest of incorporating children. This model is not analogous. Adults are not divine-like, and the two natures of Christ are of course not divisible in this way. Instead, we use the model of Christ's kenotic emptying as a quality of unity marked by giving oneself over to the other in ways that serve without destroying. Paul describes the lesson of kenosis as Christ's humility teaching the church to elevate others. Were adults to work at regarding children as better than themselves and to limit (selfish) ambition, as the apostle exhorts, they would be modeling the divestment of power that Christ models in his own incorporation of humanity in general.

Presence

Children's increased participation enhances the work of the Spirit in the life of the church. By participation, we mean that children are unified with the whole and recognized as distinct in their personhood, capacities, and culture. Recognizing children in their unique capacities requires that the dominant culture of adults exhibit presence to the less dominant one of children. Presence, as we see in the divine communion, is making room for the other. While adults may be inclusive, this inclusivity rarely reflects the diversity of children as a genuine aspect of the culture. Rather, it is usually appears in forms such as that of the men who sought, with good intent, to evangelize Willie Jennings and his mother. As it pertains to worship, children's participation becomes a reflection of adult participation as opposed to authentic, childlike participation. Thus, children often become "little adults" instead of "little children" in their own right. Or they are idealized "little children" as portrayed in the whimsical—and in fact

38. Ibid., 2.

demeaning—photography of Ann Geddes.[39] One can imagine the children echoing Jennings: "Why did they not know us?"

Incorporating children in the body means overcoming the tendency to treat them as objects of control (power) and instead to see them as wonders, alongside whom adults find their place. A helpful distinction is that between problems and mysteries. In the descriptions of Gabriel Marcel, problems have solutions, and they can be addressed with resources or the right techniques.[40] Mysteries, on the other hand, transcend solutions and techniques. Mysteries draw one into open landscapes and involvement. While a problem can be solved and one can move on, the more one ponders a mystery, the more one becomes involved with—indeed present to—it.

In philosopher James K. A. Smith's *Imagining the Kingdom*, he underscores how mystery is experienced rather than solved by relaying a memorable scene from the Jane Campion film *Bright Star*, a cinematic portrayal of the life of the poet John Keats. In it, Keats's love interest, Fanny Brawne, laments her lack of poetic understanding:

> "I still don't know how to work out a poem," Fanny confesses. Keats quietly replies with a halting soliloquy, "A poem needs understanding through the senses," he begins. "The point of diving in a lake is not immediately to swim to the shore but to be *in* the lake, to luxuriate in the sensation of the water. You do not work the lake out. It is an experience beyond thought. Poetry soothes and emboldens the soul to accept mystery." "I love mystery," Fanny replies meekly, back on her heels after the outpouring.[41]

Mystery, like poetry, is not a puzzle to be solved but a presence to be experienced. The Trinity is such a mystery, through which it is easy to imagine transcendence and open-endedness as opposed to a problem that can be solved.

Children are mysteries as well. Church historian Martin Marty has written on the importance of treating children as such. His interest in writing about children is that while they are deeply embedded in history, children make rare appearances in history books. Children have played

39. London photographer Lee Goldup has photographed adults in the kind of outlandish poses and situations that Geddes uses for children. The effect is both disturbing and illuminating.

40. Marcel, *The Mystery of Being*.

41. Smith, *Imagining the Kingdom*, 47.

significant roles in history, but historians and recorders have not envisioned them as "the agents, the makers of history and actors in it."[42] Marty addresses the power of the adult world and writes about his own work on the child as "a compensatory token that recognizes my own past neglect."[43] As mysteries, children are subjects of wonder, and, as those who spend time with children can attest, children transcend set ways of doing things and patterns of control. Treating children as mystery allows adults to engage the difficult process of being present to children as adults enter the world of the child on the child's terms. Care, rather than control, allows the mystery and wonder of the child to ground their participation and differentiation.

Care is akin to the presence of the three persons of the Godhead toward each other. As a simple example, I (Michelle) have a nephew named Johnny. Johnny often imagines he is armed with a gun, which he enjoys shooting. In the past, I have tended to treated this behavior as a problem. "Bang, bang, bang," Johnny yells. "Johnny," I begin. "Guns are bad. They are violent, and they kill people. Stop shooting me and go play with your Legos." Being a moral theologian, I am sure that I have taught Johnny a very important ethical lesson about how the world works. To boot, the problem of Johnny shooting at people is solved—at least until the next time he decides to pull out his make-believe weapon. As he obediently goes to play with his Legos, I move on to the next thing.

Treating Johnny as a problem buys me momentary peace, but, as I have learned, he still pulls out his make-believe gun. I have begun to try to be present to Johnny in a way that honors the world of his imagination. "Bang, bang, bang," Johnny yells. "Oh! You got me!" I cry out as I fall to the ground. More shooting occurs. "Johnny," I whisper loudly over his popping. "You hit me. Three times." Johnny searches for my wounds. "Johnny," I plead, "Run and get me a medic!" Quickly switching gears, Johnny makes loud siren noises and runs around the living room. "Hurry!" I urge. I actually start believing I am in pain. At that moment, Johnny decides *he* will be the medic, and he descends upon me ready to stitch the wounds and save my life.

The difference in these scenarios is significant. In the former, the adult appears to have everything under control, and the problem of Johnny playing with guns is expeditiously resolved. In the latter, the adult enters the world of the child in such a way that the child is able to participate in his

42. Marty, *The Mystery of the Child*, 8.
43. Ibid., 9.

own formation. In scenario one, the shooter put his gun away. In scenario two, the child is invited into the action long enough for the shooter-child to become a medic-child.

When adults are present to the world of children, children have space to practice their identity. It also encourages unity through participation. Such participation is incredibly difficult, and Marty suggests that adults must learn to play with children. Play takes into account such things as presence, responsiveness, freedom, and boundaries. The unity and activity of play mirrors the notions of hypostases and perichoresis in the Godhead. German theologian Karl Rahner interprets the usual translation of "master workman" as "a little child" in Proverbs 8.

> When he established the heavens, I was there, . . . when he marked out the foundations of the earth, then I was beside him, like a little child; and I was daily his delight, rejoicing before him always, rejoicing in his inhabited world and delighting in the [human race].[44]

Interpreting Rahner, Marty emphasizes the play within God's being as God's eternal connection with childhood as it determines the worth, or identity, of the other.

Children's distinctiveness warrants more than mere recognition—it should be honored and supported in ways that cultivate their growth and differentiation as child worshipers. This, we imagine, is a reflection of the unity in difference in the Godhead and an example of the kind of presence that God exhibits in God's own life.

Conclusion

This chapter has utilized Trinitarian and Christological categories to frame the phenomenon of unity in difference and the importance of incorporation. Incorporation is about close relationship, mutuality, self-giving, and becoming oneself through the other. In addition, we have examined questions of identity and differentiation as they inform the ways the Christian church might better imagine children's place in the life of the church. As members of the body of Christ, children are integral to the incorporating work of the church. Incorporation on a human level mimics God's incorporated life by striving for close relationship. Christ exhibits power, and the triune community models presence. Together these shape the work of the

---

44. Rahner quoted in Marty, *The Mystery of the Child*, 131.

body as it incorporates the kind of difference that children embody. We will return to these themes in the second half of the book.

The hypostatic union within the Trinity and Christ's two natures and the perichoretic activity of the Godhead are more than just technical ideas attempting to describe God's life as three-in-one. The very existence of these descriptive and orthodox categories for God offers an important aspect of the incorporating work of the church. Specifically, incorporation that mirrors God's triune life maintains, appreciates, and even glorifies the distinct persons within the human community *and* the unique differentiation that is the potential of each. Instead of perceiving diversity and differentiation as threat, the good news for Christ's church is that differentiation is the very mode of God's saving work, and indeed a childlike mark of the kingdom!

Children
Worship
Incorporation
Virtue
Vocation
Vision

4. Virtue

Children are well versed in the liturgy of their parents. "Shhhh," whispers many a parent to the child who is crumpling paper, banging crayons, or talking noisily during church. "Sit still!" comes naturally to parents of the young boy who is fidgeting, crawling under the pew, or making faces at the newcomers seated behind him. "Pay attention!" reprimands another parent whose daughter is writing notes to her friend. Urgent requests such as these are particularly pronounced during special music, sermons, and communion. Conversely, the peacefully worshiping parents are those whose children are sufficiently occupied or, ideally, sleeping. One can hardly argue that the child more akin to the still waters of Psalm 23 is much more welcome in worship than the child who embodies Psalm 150's imagery of praising God with loud, clanging cymbals!

The contrast between the still, quiet child and the one loudly clanging cymbals raises the question of what exactly parents, pastors, and congregations hope for the children in their midst. Is the hope that children do not distract other worshipers? Or that children will pick up the faith simply by being surrounded by Christians? Is it that the adults get everything they can out of a service with little thought to the child among them? Is the "good" child the one who is most quiet and least disruptive or possibly the child who is not present in the service at all? Most parents and adults would probably agree that excellent worship has very little to do with sitting still and being quiet, yet these are the behaviors that adults frequently reinforce and even reward in children.

If, as we discussed in chapters 2 and 3, good worship is about engaging in the triune God through the unity of the worshiping body, then the goods and ends for adults in worship directly connect with the goods and ends for children in worship. It is good that the whole worshiping community, including children and adults, is engaged in worship of the triune God. It is good for the whole worshiping community to develop virtues for Christian living. And it is good when the whole worshiping community finds itself filled with God's power and presence. In light of these desires, we assert that children do not pose *barriers* to good worship, but they actually have much potential to *facilitate* excellent worship on the part of the whole congregation.

The topic of this and the following chapter—virtues as they pertain to children in worship—might lead the reader to think that our concern is how to cultivate virtue *in* children. While that is indeed our hope, it is incomplete for two reasons. First, the ends of worship are not the cultivation of virtue. As mentioned earlier, we agree with Will Willimon's argument that virtue is a byproduct of good worship, because worship has its own intrinsic value and is its own reward.[1] In his discussion of the ends of worship, Willimon argues that the primary purpose of worship is to praise and give glory to God. The subversive function of worship is that it helps worshipers envision a new order. In other words, liturgy creates a social world for the church that forms it to see and be shaped anew, reorienting us to the deep love of neighbor.[2] Willimon's work protects against ideas that worship is utilitarian, or serves a human function, and we keep this forewarning in mind as we develop virtue and worship in this chapter.

Second, we argue that the virtues children readily acquire and distinctively embody are more than simply transforming for the child. Children's virtue in worship serves the adults in the congregation as well. Children embody virtues in ways that are distinctive to childhood and adolescence, and they also readily embody aspects of the Christian faith that are more difficult for adults. Children's practice of virtue has the capacity to push the entirety of the worshiping community more deeply into unity with God and with one another.

1. Willimon, *Service of God*, 22.
2. Ibid., 51.

We turn to virtue in the Christian tradition, including some of its strengths and flaws, to ground our assertion that children's virtue facilitates good worship for the whole body. In our analysis of virtue, we draw strongly from the work of Alasdair MacIntyre to situate virtue in the realm of social practices. We claim that worship is the primary social practice of the church and use MacIntyre's framework to examine worship as a social practice. We articulate the virtues that are intrinsic—or necessary—to the practice of worship and describe in detail how those virtues support excellent worship.

Virtue and the Christian Tradition

In the Christian moral tradition, virtue theory plays an integral role. The primary questions virtue theory raises include questions of identity and the desire to become a particular kind of person. For example, the Greek philosopher Aristotle argues that the paragon of virtue was the Athenian gentleman. Such a person achieves a constellation of many virtues including the intellectual qualities of understanding, technological skill, wisdom, and prudence, along with the moral virtues of courage, temperance, and justice. Church father St. Augustine includes some of these virtues in his description of a moral exemplar whose distinguishing quality is love of God and neighbor, in that order. For him, virtues are defined in ways that build on the supreme virtue of charity, and the one who embodies charity is virtuous because her acts refer back to her maker.

Following Aristotle and Augustine, medieval theologian Thomas Aquinas contributes the significant Christian category of theological or supernatural virtues: faith, hope, and love. In his view, the most virtuous person in this life exhibits wisdom, or contemplation of the divine, and enjoys friendship as it mirrors union with the divine. The medieval mystic St. Bonaventure, a contemporary of Aquinas, slightly shifts the focus of virtue and describes it in terms of the "potential excellence of things."[3] By seeing virtue in the created world, human beings are illumined with knowledge of God. Bonaventure's paradigm of virtue, then, calls moral exemplars to be other-oriented. Bonaventure evokes a kind of reverence for seeking the natural ends of all things and awe for the human and the non-human creation.

Each of these seminal thinkers in the area of virtue offers much to the Christian ethical tradition and moral formation. However, the focus is

3. Bonaventure, *The Soul's Journey into God*, 64.

largely on character traits and static categories for understanding how one becomes a moral exemplar. Classic formulations of virtue can be summarily defined as excellences of character cultivated over time through habit. Such a definition introduces a formal splitting off of habits from excellences, though they are related. The definition also begs the question of whether virtues are ends, as traditionally thought, or merely aspects of a larger framework of meaning and action that not only constitutes "ethical moments" but also changes through time and culture. For example, does Aristotle's constellation of virtues encompass all of the traits necessary for dealing with ethical issues in the global South? Do the practices through which Christians cultivate or receive faith, hope, and love matter in a given historical period? How are particular ways that the virtuous person enacts justice important in the context of Christianity in North America? Does power play a role in the connection between humility and faith?

Christian ethicist Miguel De La Torre argues that virtue theory remains trapped in a white, middle-class ethic and that the substance of virtue theory continues to be defined by those in power.[4] In connecting social location with objective, universal truth, De La Torre identifies inherent problems within virtue theory as it has emerged from groups of privilege. He concludes that the attainment of virtue historically is classist and derives from the dominant culture's significant resources for engaging in moral reflection. Moreover, the virtue ethic of Euro-Americans is one that focuses on personal piety as opposed to a reality more fundamental to marginalized groups—namely that of survival.

De La Torre's critique of Euro-American virtue theory is well founded and largely justified. Moreover, he offers a promising avenue to reflect on virtue as it pertains to childhood. His critique falls short, however, when he considers the ambiguous nature of survival ethics or ethics from the underside. Specifically, he notes that underprivileged groups or persons are forced to make choices between bad decisions and worse decisions. He uses the example of stealing in antebellum America, noting that virtue theory traditionally deems stealing as immoral.

Yet, most virtue theory approaches moral questions based on the virtues that are embodied—not, as De La Torre's argument suggests, through categories of rights or law. Rather, virtue theory examines morality based on a particular *character trait* one has acquired (or not). His argument breaks down when he neglects to analyze whether the action of stealing for

---

4. De La Torre, "Doing Latina/o Ethics from the Margins of Empire," 8.

subsistence is habitual and how the action is connected with a character trait. For example, is stealing an action resulting from the prideful desire to attain goods for self-betterment? Or, is the theft an action resulting from the (wise) character trait of acting on behalf of one's own or one's children's survival? These examples offer two very different contexts for analyzing action. They also reveal that virtue analyses inherently entail ambiguity, unlike deontological approaches that tend to lack moral ambiguity or utilitarian ones that require only exacting calculations. While De La Torre is insightful in drawing attention to the bad decision/worse decision challenge, he does not fully recognize the capacity *in theory* for virtue ethics to address adequately the underprivileged exemplar.

The strengths and flaws of De La Torre's critique offer much insight to the context of children and virtue. Character excellences in Christian moral formation favor those in power, namely adults, and neglect a significant focus on describing virtues in ways that children may more readily embody. The idea that one cultivates virtue over time, while true, can also have the effect of overlooking virtues embodied by children. In the best of worlds, the character of the child transforms over time, as it does with adults. However, childhood is not limited to formation for the future, and children often have virtuous character traits and actions before they reach maturity. De La Torre's critique about who decides which virtues are important and how they are embodied is exceedingly relevant.

Conversely, the blind spots in his argument expose two important points as we consider children in worship. First, the action of the boy making faces at the adults behind him during worship initially appears disruptive. On the other hand, it may have emerged from the boy's capacity for love and to be loved. Unlike many adults, the boy does not consider connection with a new person a risk, and in his case, making faces is actually an opportunity to make the people laugh—assuming, of course, that they are open to the boy's antics. The unintentional consequence might be that these newcomers receive the message that they are a part of things, welcomed into the congregation in a small but powerful way because they are noticed.

Second, character traits cannot be statically defined. The virtues of faith, hope, and love, for example, have different forms and contours. The boy's capacity for love as demonstrated in silly faces appears very different than the adult's, who demonstrates capacity through a handshake or an invitation to lunch. Both, however, have potential to contribute to the good of welcoming the stranger. In sum, the question of actions as they are linked with virtue and constitute *part of* virtue offer much to this conversation, as do the particular and multifaceted *ways* that virtues are actually embodied.

Virtue and Social Practices

In *After Virtue,* Alasdair McIntyre examines broad social practices as they constitute the virtuous person. Rather than simply analyzing how certain actions line up with particular virtues, he defines virtue in the context of social practices. He claims that the good life for such-and-such a person grounds the particular virtues that a culture or theory advances. Virtue itself is a secondary concept that exists subsequent to an understanding of the good life and one's place in it. The primary ground for articulating virtue, then, is the "concept of *what anyone filling such-and-such a role ought to do.*"[5] MacIntyre's grounding of virtue offers a helpful answer to De La Torre's critiques in that knowing and accessing virtue is necessitated by knowing and accessing the social roles and environment that inform virtue. In other words, an objective set of virtues devoid of social contexts and practices does not exist.

MacIntyre's analysis explains the foundation of virtue in three stages. The first, and most important for our study, is the notion of a social practice. A practice provides the primary arena for construing virtue. MacIntyre defines a practice as:

> any coherent and complex form of socially established coopera-
> tive human activity through which goods internal to that form of
> activity are realized in the course of trying to achieve those stan-
> dards of excellence which are appropriate to, and partially defini-
> tive of, that form of activity, with the result that human powers to
> achieve excellence, and human conceptions of the ends and goods
> involved, are systematically extended.[6]

MacIntyre's lengthy definition introduces a few pressing points. Cooperative human activities, or social practices, have sufficient complexity and history. They are multifaceted and have a variety of dimensions. Social practices also have rules and standards of excellence. These standards constitute the rubrics for determining specific goods that are definitive of the practice and a measure for whether these goods are achieved. While stable

5. MacIntyre, *After Virtue,* 184.
6. Ibid., 187.

and objective, the rules, standards, and goods may change or transform over time through evolutions on the part of the practitioners.

MacIntyre also distinguishes external from internal goods. External goods tend to be material things that can be possessed. They may mark excellence in practice but are not inherently related to the practice. Examples include trophies, ribbons, money, public recognition, and other prizes. They also tend to be defined by scarcity, in that there is a limited supply of external kinds of goods. Internal goods, on the other hand, are inherently related to the practice and *must be achieved* in order for a practice to fit within agreed upon standards of excellence. Moreover, the only way internal goods are achieved is by engaging in the practice itself. In a moment, we will look more in depth at worship as a social practice. Suffice it to say here that an external good of worship might be recognition or status (e.g., for such accomplishments as eloquent preaching, beautiful architecture, or excellence in music). An external good might also be as simple as offering candy to a child as a reward for sitting still (or, better, for worshiping well!). An internal good to worship might be joy experienced by participating in singing or by preaching an inspiring sermon (when no one notices). An internal good might be appreciation for one's brother who comes to the table for bread or the sense of peace that comes from reconciliation with God in confession.

Another aspect of social practices that MacIntyre considers is the institutional aspect, especially as related to external and internal goods. MacIntyre makes clear that practices and institutions ought not be conflated or confused.[7] Preaching, for example, is a practice. The church is an institution.[8] He argues that institutions are necessarily interested in external goods because they need resources such as money, power, and other material goods in order to sustain themselves over time. Indeed, a social practice needs a stable institution for its very survival. MacIntyre notes that because of the intimate and necessary relationship between institutions and practices, all social practices are vulnerable to the corresponding institution's tendency to sustain itself with external goods. In his words, social practices are "vulnerable to the competitiveness of the institution."[9] Social

7. Ibid., 194.

8. In naming the church as an institution, we refer to such aspects as governance, organization, structure, etc. We hold simultaneously that the church is more than an institution—it is mystical body, community of disciples, herald of good news, etc.

9. MacIntyre, *After Virtue*, 194.

practices within an institution play an invaluable role, then, in resisting the mere acquisition or accumulation of goods necessary for sustenance. Social practices provide the arena for virtue, excellence, and the achieving of goods *internal to* and *definitive of* the practice, therefore in no small part contributing to the institutions in which they function.

The last key aspect of MacIntyre's understanding of social practices is their capacity to transform or enrich the community. This kind of cultivation that occurs beyond the confines of the practice itself is what MacIntyre means by "systematically extended." Social practices are not about personal preferences or gain. Rather, they comprise those aspects of life that are ongoing and sustain communities. In this way, practices are more than techniques or performances because they are imbued with meaning and context that shape and situate activity within larger narrative accounts.

The narrative aspect of the foundation of virtue is the second stage of MacIntyre's analysis. The complexity of narrative within the whole of MacIntyre's work renders it beyond the scope of this study; however, one point is critical for our purposes. MacIntyre claims that a deciding element of achieving goods that are internal to a social practice is the dimension of what it means to live as one who *is* a social practitioner. In other words, the practitioner not only achieves goods in the context of engaging in the social practice. She also lives her life in some way that is related to the social practice. Practicing something well and beautifully in some way shapes the life of the practitioner.

We have explored some of the more notable characteristics of MacIntyre's analysis of a social practice. They are complex, yet coherent, historically established activities. They have objective standards of excellence that are subject to change. They have recognizable goods intrinsic to their practice. They are situated in institutions and vulnerable to them. Finally, they enrich communities and contribute to narratives of individuals and communities.

Worship as a Social Practice

The practice of Christian worship fits well into MacIntyre's parameters of a social practice. In his article, "Liturgy and Ethics: Something Old, Something New," theologian Stephen Wilson discusses the central aspects of MacIntyre's description of social practices as they apply to worship.[10] First,

10. Wilson, "Liturgy and Ethics," 24–45.

worship has an inherent complexity and coherency within the specific liturgical rite, as well as through the history of the church's worship practices, rituals, and paradigms. Within specific rites, there are many different complex words and actions spoken that all move toward a coherent end. For example, Wilson notes that the rite of baptism is complex in its prayer over the waters, vows taken by the baptizand and congregation, prayer of blessing, the act of washing with water, etc. Nevertheless, the rite moves toward the coherent end of incorporating the baptizand into the body of Christ.[11] Similarly, Wilson argues that the main components of worship—word and table—while complex and evolving, have remained a central and coherent part of the liturgical life of the church over the past 2,000 years. Worship is a social practice in its complexity and cohesiveness.

Worship also fits the paradigm of a social practice because it is truly social and cooperative. Contrary to the distortion of worship that often portrays it as the work between an individual and God, Christian worship at its roots is a social activity. Liturgy (*leitourgia*) is the "work of the people," and by its very nature, worship is a practice that requires a group of people to gather together.[12] Naturally, such a social construct requires cooperation. For the pastors and lay leaders, this cooperation involves careful and thoughtful planning of the service and its logistics, clear instructions for the community to follow, engagement in leadership during singing, proclamation of the word, presiding at the sacraments, etc. For the congregation, cooperation requires faithful attendance, active participation in singing, responsive readings and prayers, and the various bodily movements of the liturgy (i.e., standing, singing, kneeling, coming forward for communion). As an individual gives herself over to the norms and rules that are part of any given worship service, worship becomes truly social and collaborative, a practice that forms both the individual and the community through its unique activity.

Other aspects of worship fit MacIntyre's parameters, beyond those which Wilson names in his analysis. Worship is also a social practice because it is a practice situated within the institution of the church. On the macro level, this can be witnessed in the organizational structures of various denominations. Such structures, while not disinterested in the internal goods of the worshiping life of the church, by their very nature (especially in the more hierarchical Catholic and Episcopal traditions)

11. Ibid., 32.
12. Ibid., 31.

concern themselves with the external goods of the church: money, order, and governance. On the micro level, each local church is an institution in which the social practice of worship takes place in the context of organization and programs, broadly speaking.

While the practice of worship forms the heart of the church, the external goods with their bills, bylaws, and infrastructure are also vital for worship to take place. Institutions are necessarily concerned with external goods—the acquisition and accumulation of goods—for their survival and longevity. Yet worship as a social practice seeks after internal goods that do not always line up with the external goods of the institutional church. Indeed, if hearing the words proclaimed by Jesus to give all our money to the poor were taken seriously, what would that do to the tithes and offerings and the church budget? We argue that worship, as the social practice that defines the Christian community, ought to play a prophetic role in the life of the institutional church, pushing even the necessary organizational structures and ecclesial hierarchies to follow the cruciform pattern of Christ. Or, to put it more simply, the institutional church exists for the good of the worshiping community and not the other way around.[13]

Finally, the social practice of worship has potential to transform and enrich the world beyond the practice of worship. We take up this theme more directly in chapter 6 as it relates to the ways worship forms the community of faith to live excellently. Here we note that the narrative identity that shapes believers in worship, along with the practice of virtue that is rehearsed in worship, cultivates characters who have a mission in the world.[14] This mission, as we outline in the final chapter, is based on the character of worship but is not limited to worship. As we argued in chapter 1, worship portrays the world as it *really* is—full of God's loving activity. Systematically extending God's love beyond the portals of the church enriches the world in profound ways.

13. MacIntyre notes, "if in a particular society the pursuit of external goods were to become dominant, the concept of virtues might suffer first attrition and then perhaps something near total effacement, although simulacra might abound" (*After Virtue*, 196).

14. For an excellent analysis on the narrative shaping of identity in worship, see Wilson, "Liturgy and Ethics."

Internal Goods of Worship

Is there such a thing as excellent worship? We claim that excellence in worship is important for Christian communities who take seriously the idea that worship is central to identity. The practice of worship is excellent when it achieves the goods that are internal to and therefore defining of worship, and we explore those in this section.

While the practice of worship could rightly lay claim to a myriad of internal goods, we agree with liturgist Don Saliers that the fundamental internal goods of worship—or, as Saliers calls them, the "double focus of worship"—are the "glorification of God and the sanctification of [hu] man[ity]."[15] These internal goods fit the criteria set by MacIntyre. First, both the glorification of God and the sanctification of humanity can only be achieved properly in the context of worship or activities like it.[16] Corporate worship is indeed one of the few times in which Christians set aside all other activities for the express purpose of glorifying God cooperatively, and in the presence of God (*coram Deo*) made known in word and sacrament, we are transformed into the likeness of the God we serve. This double focus is glorification and sanctification.

Similarly, the glorification of God and sanctification of humanity are not part of a zero-sum game or subject to scarcity. Akin to God's own glory, human glorification knows no limits and is only enriched by voices added in praise of the triune God. In the same way, one person's increased sanctification does not take away from a limited storehouse of sanctity; it is quite the opposite. As George MacDonald remarked in his fairytale *The Princess and Curdie*, "there is a capillary attraction in the facing of two souls, that lifts faith beyond the level to which either could raise it alone."[17] As it is with faith, so it is with sanctification. In the worshiping community we are sanctified "beyond the level" achievable alone, and our individual growth

15. Saliers, "Liturgy and Ethics," 183. This is also the Catholic definition of worship promulgated by Pope Pius X in his *Motu Proprio, Tra le Sollecitudini* ("Instruction on Sacred Music") when he asserts, "Sacred music, being a complementary part of the solemn liturgy, participates in the general scope of the liturgy, which is the glory of God and the sanctification and edification of the faithful." Wilson in "Liturgy and Ethics" also uses the glorification of God and sanctification of humanity as two internal goods of worship but adds a third: "communion" (32).

16. Wilson, "Liturgy and Ethics," uses the example of "corporal acts of mercy" as one similar activity in which glorification and sanctification can be achieved (32). Corporate prayer might be another example.

17. MacDonald, *The Princess and Curdie*, 72.

in sanctification serves to assist other individuals and the community as a whole toward holiness. In these ways the glorification of God and the sanctification of humanity are foundational goods internal to the social practice of worship.

Moreover, to achieve excellence worship requires both the glorification of God and sanctification of humanity simultaneously. If worship is only glorification of God without sanctification, we cannot be glorifying the Christian God embodied in Jesus Christ who lived in union with the Father and Spirit. Jesus of Nazareth's faith was always an embodied one, lived out in personal piety, prayer, and devotion to the Father. Jesus' life also included the corollary works of feeding the hungry, opening the eyes of the blind, and healing the afflicted. Riffing off James, worship without works is dead. Furthermore, attempting sanctification without the glorification of God easily devolves into a self-help effort deprived of the power of the triune God. Neither glorification nor sanctification alone comprises the whole of Christian worship. Worship professor Christian Scharen claims, "The issue is not 'reducing' worship to its social and ethical effects; rather, given the claims made about the formative power of liturgy and the inherent ethical character of the life of Christian discipleship, Christian worship logically entails social and ethical effects."[18] Glorification and sanctification are always two sides of the same coin of worship.

Glorification of God

It would be easy to assume that both the glorification of God and the sanctification of humanity are present in any Christian worship service, but a service whose songs and prayers consist primarily of "I" language along with a sermon of moral exhortation does not fulfill the deeper meanings of glorification and sanctification. This begs the question: what then do we mean by the glorification of God and the sanctification of humanity? It is our contention that the glorification of God in worship consists of: 1) rehearsing the redemptive story of God; 2) speaking truthfully about God; and 3) giving thick descriptions of God.

First, the glorification of God requires the rehearsal of God's redemptive story. As we discussed in chapter 2, worship is God-centered and storied. Yet, it is worth reaffirming the centrality that God and God's redemptive story centered on the birth, life, death, resurrection, and ascension of Jesus

18. Scharen, "Lois, Liturgy, and Ethics," 281.

Christ plays in worship. Throughout the biblical narrative, worship consists of telling the great and marvelous deeds of God. When the Hebrew people miraculously escape from the Egyptians through the Red Sea, Miriam composes a song on the shoreline and leads the people in recounting God's mighty acts in delivering them from bondage. Once the people have entered the land, they are told to bring their first fruits of the harvest to God, reciting the story of God choosing Abraham through their deliverance from captivity (Deut 26:1–10). The Psalter, that great hymnic storehouse of both the Jewish people and the church, fills the space of prayer by recounting God's great works of creation, judgment, and deliverance. The Passover festival liturgically retells of God's redemptive work, year after year. Finally, in the Passover meal with his disciples, Jesus reinterprets the bread and the cup to tell the story of his life, death, and resurrection until he comes again. We rehearse this story every time we gather at the table. The recitation of God's redemptive story is indeed the biblical framework for worship, and it is carried into the great tradition of the church through the recitation of creeds, Eucharistic prayers, and the centrality of hearing from God's word. Thus, worship that glorifies God centers on God's story and invites the individual and the community to enter the grand and all-pervading narrative of God.

Worship that glorifies God is not only centered on the redemptive story of God, it also speaks truthfully about God. This may seem obvious, yet often in practice our worship speaks falsities about God's person and work. The children's sermon that compares the Trinity to an egg or water (modalism),[19] the song that notes, "we rise up from the ashes to create ourselves anew" (Pelagianism),[20] and the prayer at a funeral thanking God for the soul's escape from the body to an ethereal heaven in the sky (Gnostic dualism)[21] all distort the truth about the triune God. Within our own denomination (the Evangelical Covenant Church), we have commu-

---

19. Modalism, or Sabellianism, is the belief that the persons of God are merely different features of God rather than eternally present as part of God's triune being. In other words, each appears in different form, but not as three in one. This view was deemed heretical, specifically in the Athanasian Creed in the late fourth century.

20. Pelagianism teaches the goodness of human capacities as they have potential to move us to God. This view was condemned at a council in Carthage (418) and again at the Council of Ephesus (431) for rejecting the power of God's grace for salvation.

21. Gnosticism is the belief that some have special knowledge of salvation and that the quest for knowledge entails a hatred of the body and material reality. Irenaeus of Lyons (125–202) was a primary champion against this heresy.

nally rejected a penal substitutionary view of the atonement that sets God's wrath above God's love and divides the Godhead between a wrathful Father and a loving Son. Yet we have noted many congregations who proudly sing the second stanza of "In Christ Alone": "'Til on that cross as Jesus died, / the wrath of God was satisfied." This either shows a lack of care in planning worship or a disregard for the honesty and integrity of our words in worship. In order to glorify God, we must proclaim words of truth in our worship.

Beyond avoiding falsities, worship glorifies God by offering thick descriptions of the God we worship. Anthropologist Clifford Geertz employs thick descriptions as rich language that includes not only what is observed, but also the background of the subject, person, or group of focus. Thick descriptions engage symbolism, narrative, and webs of meaning.[22] Often, however, congregations settle on one image of God that is readily observable and speaks to them. Examples include God the Father as angry judge, Jesus as buddy, and the Holy Spirit as wonder worker.

Another example is worship that engages only one person of the Trinity. These partial truths are limiting and can easily become the god of worship, creating in effect an idol out of one attribute or image of God. Speaking to the depth of God's character in all of its fullness and paradox is central to glorifying God. God is the Creator of the vast cosmos, fully transcendent and forever hidden from our knowledge. God is also the one who is revealed in Jesus and calls us friends, intimately immanent to creation. God is found both in the tragedy and senselessness of the crucifixion as well as in the unexpected joy of the resurrection—in hopeless lament and unbridled praise. God is made known in the cacophony of the noise and chaos of our lives but also speaks in the deep and sustained silences. Similarly, thick descriptions of God require that we speak of God in worship as a triune God—eternally Three-in-One, Christ as fully human and fully divine, and the Holy Spirit as the breath of God who is, as the Nicene Creed acclaims, "the Lord and giver of life." To glorify God, we must proclaim the redemptive story of the triune God honestly, in all of its depth and grandeur, brokenness and paradox. It is then that the glorification of God truly fulfills its role as an internal good, spurring the social practice of worship toward excellence.

22. Geertz, *Local Knowledge*, ix. I borrow the connection between thick descriptions and liturgy from historian Phillip J. Anderson's "Mystic Chords of Memory."

Sanctification of Humanity

Defining the sanctification of humanity through worship is complex. One might define sanctification as it emerges from the acts of prayer, Bible study, devotion, and works of compassion, mercy, and justice that take place outside of the context of corporate worship. In chapter 6, we argue that these actions are manifestations of the practice of worship as it is "systematically extended" in our day-to-day lives. The "liturgy after the liturgy," as the Orthodox call it, includes the ways that worship, as the heart of the Christian faith, enriches the community and narratives that surround it. Within worship itself, however, there also exist liturgical elements that enact the transformative power of faith and can help us grasp what we mean by liturgical sanctification. Primarily, these elements are the confession of sin and assurance of pardon, the passing of the peace, intercessory prayer, and the sacraments.[23] Not only do these elements enact sanctification, but they also provide the symbolic tools for systematically extending their particular messages of sanctification out into the world.

The confession of sin and assurance of pardon are among the more obvious ways sanctification is enacted in worship. When entering the presence of a holy God as worshipers, we are made starkly aware of our own brokenness and sin: "Woe is me! I am lost, for I am a person of unclean lips, living among a people of unclean lips; yet my eyes have seen the King, the Lord of hosts!" (Isa 6:5). In individual and corporate confessions of sin, Christians acknowledge that we allow stories of materialism, nationalism, and the American Dream, for example, to shape our lives—rather than being inhabited by the all-encompassing and redemptive story of God. Stories not only shape our lives; they affect our actions and relationships. Confession truthfully confronts allegiances that compete with allegiance to God. The outcome is not the experience of guilt or shame. Rather, it is a transformed person.

As Isaiah envisions, the telos of confession is forgiveness and reconciliation with God: "Then one of the seraphs flew to me, holding a live coal that had been taken from the altar with a pair of tongs. The seraph touched my mouth with it and said: 'Now that this has touched your lips, your guilt has departed and your sin is blotted out'" (Isa 6:6–7). Just as God sanctifies Isaiah through confession and the assurance of pardon so that he may participate in God's mission in the world, so God sanctifies the faithful

---

23. See chapter 2 for the deeper implications of the sacraments in worship.

through their confession of sin and the assurance of pardon. By admitting our brokenness, we open ourselves to receive the transforming grace of God that enacts sanctification and frees us for mission.

Having been reconciled with God, forgiven people are freed to forgive others and enact God's reconciliation in all interpersonal relationships. This is ritualized in many congregations through the passing of the peace. When the rite of reconciliation remains connected with Jesus' words to the disciples in John's Gospel, the greeting "peace be with you" is a bold enactment of the reconciling work of Christ. It is diluted beyond recognition when it is reduced to greeting neighbors and making brunch plans. Reconciliation is an integral moment of transformed relationships, and the people who surround us in the congregation (including our family!) are the same broken, resentful, and reconciled people who have also confessed their sins and received the unearned forgiveness of God. Having been reconciled to God through God's unmerited grace, people live out the sanctifying power of the Holy Spirit—a work in which humans participate—by effecting reconciliation with one another. Although the passing of the peace may be only the beginning of the difficult work of deep reconciliation, the rite represents the conciliatory Christian spirit first witnessed in God's own redemptive work and the ongoing forgiveness of the people of God. Reconciliation thus becomes a way of life for those grounded in the story of God through the routine, or habit, of liturgy.

Another way worshipers enact sanctification in liturgy is through intercessory prayer. In praying for the needs of the broader community and world, worshipers are first reminded that the work of the world's sanctification cannot be carried out through sheer human effort or will. Intercessory prayer recognizes that the faithful act as God's coworkers until the full redemption of creation is completed in the eschaton. Furthermore, intercessory prayer for others enacts a focus on the other(s) that removes the pray-ers from the center of the world's story and recalls the other-centered work of Christ who gave his life for the life of the world. Through intercessory prayer, Christians are reminded of the call God has placed on their lives to be Christ's hands and feet and to use their resources to ameliorate the suffering of others. Intercessory prayer necessarily leads to intercessory action, or justice, on behalf of others for the sake of the kingdom of God.

In these three aforementioned liturgical acts that represent the entire liturgy, along with the unifying effects of baptism and communion as discussed in chapter 2, Christians practice individual and communal sanctification. Sanctification's fruits enacted in worship are by nature and definition "systematically extended" into their relationships, communities, nation, and world. While the end of worship is not to transform communities, the enrichment and transformation of a people are inherent to the nature and practice of worship. After all, this is what the church means by loving one's neighbor, forming disciples of Jesus Christ, and building new identities in Christ. Excellent worship that receives and participates in the sanctifying work of the Spirit necessarily enriches the lives and communities beyond the practice of worship itself.

Virtues in Worship

Thus far, we have argued that there is such a thing as excellent worship, and while worship itself is complex and takes a wide variety of forms, we maintain that worshiping communities can identify and practice excellence in worship. At the heart of excellent worship is glorification of God and sanctification of humanity, and we have discussed some of the ways Christians recognize these primary goods. Revisiting MacIntyre's description of social practices, we now offer a brief analysis of the actual virtues that cultivate glorification and sanctification. Our underlying assumption is that excellent worship as glorification and sanctification is based on ongoing transformation and growth in the worshiping community's relationship to the triune God.

The primary virtues essential to and internal to worship as a social practice are the traditional three theological virtues made known in Scripture: faith, hope, and love. Other virtues, such as the capacity for wonder, are related to these three. Thomas Aquinas describes the three theological virtues as having God as their objects and as the avenue through which followers of Christ participate in God's life.[24] In other words, the theological virtues order believers to God and dispose them to love God and neighbor in ways that human moral virtues, such as courage, do not. While faith, hope, and love are gifts from God, every act of faith, hope, and love increases the capacity to receive and enact each. They remain gifts, but they grow and develop as character traits.

Because of the complex nature of salvation and the process of God incorporating humanity into God's triune life, it goes without saying that these three virtues are themselves complex. As Miguel De La Torre points

24. Thomas Aquinas, *Summa Theologica*, Question LXII, Article 1.

out, virtues are embodied in communities in diverse and complex ways. We discuss their complexity and diversity as we analyze each. We also assume that virtues change and grow over time, as does the process of sanctification, and that because these three virtues have God as their primary object, they are necessary for cultivating the goods of glorification and sanctification in the practice of worship.

Faith

Sunday school curriculum teaches the content of Scripture's narratives. Youth education often includes indoctrination through confirmation or catechism. Adult education takes up topics in the Christian faith or interprets books of the Bible. Each of these modes of formation works with the idea that faith entails content, and further, that belief is grounded in right knowledge.

In fact, one of the primary ways in which Christians define faith is right belief. Protestants in particular focus on belief in God as the linchpin of salvation. The claim in John 3:16 that "whosoever believes in him will have eternal life" is taken to mean that assent equals salvation. Roman Catholicism also has its version of faith as belief, particularly in its catechetical formation. Belief and intellectual assent to both God and the teachings of the Christian church are important aspects of faith. Learning and affirming who God is and what God does is critical to the formation of Christian disciples. As we suggest above, it also contributes to excellent worship. However, intellectual assent does not cover the entirety of faith as it is developed in Scripture.

Faith is also a gift from God. It is not some random gift divested from God's self—it is God's gift *of* God's self. It is the divine gift that holds sanctifying and saving power, as Ephesians 2 proclaims. Moreover, faithfulness is who God is. God does not only extend grace to humanity and hope they will receive it; God also exhibits faithfulness. Throughout the biblical narrative, God extends grace even when humans are undeserving. In the aftermath of Israel's destruction by the Babylonians—one of the darkest moments in Israel's history—God's faithfulness provides sustaining power, and in the midst of lament, the poet-author of Lamentations proclaims, "The steadfast love of the Lord never ceases, his mercies never come to an end; they are new every morning; great is your faithfulness" (Lam 3:22–23).

God promises to be faithful to Israel and remains loyal to her even when she is unfaithful to God.

Faith as a gift challenges the Christian moral community to reflect on the receptive work that is the faith of humans. In an article on faith, philosopher Karl Clifton-Soderstrom contrasts faith with sloth as the vice that blocks humans' ability to cultivate and receive faith. He defines sloth not simply as the lack of meaningful activity, but rather as the inability to receive God's gifts with gratitude. It is a turning inward that paralyzes one's ability to participate in the world. Clifton-Soderstrom describes sloth as burdening one with his or her own emptiness.[25] Passion and vitality are nonexistent. He argues that receiving faith is akin to a peaceful passivity that allows God's grace to transform persons into vehicles that extend grace to others.

Peaceful passivity leads to another dimension of faith, namely trust. Luther emphasizes that the Greek word *pistis* literally means trust in the broad sense of placing one's trust in who God is and what God is doing. Giving up control yet paying attention and being vigilant to how God is working in the lives of God's people is not easy for fast-paced, twenty-first century, globalized people. However, trust is at the heart of faith as the Old and New Testaments develop faith, and as such, trust marks an important aspect of the character of faith.

Finally, the cultivation of faith rests on the capacity not only to receive but also to be thankful. The doxological nature of humans as they open themselves up to God's grace moves persons to take on a posture of receiving all that is good and of God. Many of the psalms communicate doxology as their primary message. The writers are thankful for God's goodness, for creation, for deliverance and redemption, for joy and blessings, and for other people. Thanksgiving is deeply connected with faith and the capacity for humans to be loyal to their Creator.

We offer a succinct yet multifaceted description of faith and assert that faith is a virtue essential to excellent worship and to the goods that are inherent to worship. Gift, reception, doxology, openness, transformation, assent, and trust reveal a robust notion of faith that connects with the whole movement of the liturgy. Hearing God's word, being open to the Holy Spirit in prayer, trusting that the sacraments shape participants, depending on the body to reconcile, and believing the Apostles' Creed are a few ways that faith "works" in worship. In other words, the worshiping body does the

25. Clifton-Soderstrom, "When All Things Are Wearisome," 20.

work of liturgy from the place of faith, which in turn forms and shapes the body's ability to glorify God and to be sanctified, or transformed, by God's gifts.

Hope

In the book of Genesis, Rachel is a paragon of hope. She laments her barrenness, crying, "Give me children or I will die!" Then, in a tragic and ironic twist, she dies in childbirth. Rachel gallantly names her son *ben-oni*, son of my sorrow, and breathes her last. Her hope, however, does not die. In Jeremiah, readers hear her posthumously as she weeps for her children who are no more. She has very little to stand on with God, but she continues to wail even into the Gospel of Matthew, directly into arguably the worst story in all of Scripture—the slaughter of the innocents. In the midst of this utterly hopeless situation, Rachel's hope does not take the form of comfort or escape. Her hope appears in the form of loud tears, and while faithful readers may find no comfort, they accompany Rachel in hopes that God might hear her cries.

As with faith, hope is too often stripped of its complexity and defined as optimism for the future or a vague desire for something better. Some of the petitions of day-to-day life offer evidence of cheap hope. We hope for better weather on the weekend, a good job, or the perfect mate. Cheap hope is also witnessed in escapist theologies that passively await God's salvation. Such hope treats God as the grand *Deus ex machina* who steps in at the last moment to save God's people without warning. In such a narrative, the world is bad and getting worse, the church is a refuge protecting the saints from evil, and social or environmental action is a waste of time because the world will eventually be destroyed anyway. This kind of hope is ultimately a form of despair that sees no role for humanity in the redemption of the cosmos.

Such cheap hope is found on the other end of the theological spectrum as well. Hope as an unfettered optimism, such as the view that God has a reason for everything that happens for good or ill, can blind itself to sin and evil. Distorted optimistic hope avoids sadness at all costs, at the expense of neglecting real suffering in oneself, others, and society. Avoidance, escapism, and optimism thrive in the empty platitude, the unexamined life. In the end, such a hope is devoid of deep human connection and living faith in the God who is at work in both the joys and sorrows of our world. True hope, then, is found neither in the despairing critiques of the cynic nor in the rose-colored glasses of the eternal optimist.

Christian hope is the belief that the future is in the hands of a faithful God, giving faithful people both the courage to face pain and brokenness and the strength not to be overcome by it. As Karl Clifton-Soderstrom notes, "Hope engenders the proper posture toward God, by instilling in us a patient orientation toward the word of promise that God will be faithful in the future."[26] Hope must, then, be found in the dialectic between lament and thanksgiving. Old Testament scholar James Bruckner rightly notes, "Lament is the seedbed of hope."[27] This is seen repeatedly in the biblical witness, but it is most clearly witnessed in the Psalter. In the great liturgical storehouse of the Psalms, the psalmists bring their pain, sorrow, and hatred to God in order that they may be transformed into hope. The author of Lamentations can praise and thank God in the ashes of destruction because of God's covenant promising, "I will take you as my people, and I will be your God" (Exod 6:7). Similarly, believers can praise God in the midst of the destruction of their own lives because they have been promised not only a future in the kingdom of God, but through baptism, they are children of God who participate *presently* in God's triune life. Hope knows both the cruciform and resurrection life, and both are necessary for a true hope.

Finally, hope in God's ongoing faithfulness opens the eyes of the Christian community to awe and wonder in the present. Hope as wonder and mystery is about experiencing God in the present—even believing that the present is a gift from God. Hope as presence orients one to the awe and wonder of God's good, true, and beautiful creation even in the midst of present trials and brokenness. In Marilynne Robinson's acclaimed novel *Gilead,* an aging pastor reflects on a recent Pentecost sermon he gave in his rural church.

> It has seemed to me sometimes as though the Lord breathes on this poor gray ember of Creation and it turns to radiance—for a moment or a year or the span of a life. And then it sinks back into itself again, and to look at it no one would know it had anything to do with fire, or light. That is what I said in the Pentecost sermon. I have reflected on that sermon, and there is some truth in it. But the Lord is more constant and far more extravagant than it seems to imply. Wherever you turn your eyes the world can shine like

26. Clifton-Soderstrom, "Fearful Greed and Trembling Hope," 20.

27. Bruckner, *Healthy Human Life,* 180.

transfiguration. You don't have to bring a thing to it except a little willingness to see. Only, who could have the courage to see it?[28]

The virtue of hope, as God's gift of presence made known in both lament and thanksgiving, gives worshipers the courage to be startled by beauty, awed by the cosmos, and lost in the wonder of God's extravagant and over-abundant love.

Charity

Love has many meanings and connotations, but the depth of Christian charity lies in the shared love within the triune God. Love is the name of God, and it describes the being of God, the relationship within the God-head, and the gift of love that is God in Jesus Christ. Love is the basis for all God's actions and purposes, most especially creation and redemption. Karl Clifton-Soderstrom writes, "love is not simply the greatest of the human virtues, but is *greater* than virtue itself. Love is divine."[29] The Christian God is relational at the core, and this shared life, as we discussed in chapter 3, incorporates humanity as well. Various dimensions of love are affirmed in human relationships. In describing love, we refer to the work in chapter 3 on incorporation and argue that the work of incorporating difference in unity is primarily the work of love. As with the virtues of faith and hope, love is a virtue that is rich, multidimensional, and necessary for the practice of worship.

Taking into account the broad parameters of God's love, how does love manifest itself in the human community as gift and virtue? Concisely, love, or charity, is friendship with God and, on the basis of that friendship, friendship with humanity. If relationality and love describe God's love in community, then love is what human beings are created for. The greatest command is to love, and love forms the basis for unity between people—including the body of Christ and even one's enemies. Love, in short, is a depth of relationality, acceptance, care, and mutuality. Christian love takes the form of service, showing honor, interdependence, and reciprocity. Love is patient, kind, rejoices in truth, bears all, believes all, hopes all, and endures all. Love never ends because love is God.

28. Robinson, *Gilead*, 245.
29. Clifton-Soderstrom, "Love, the Very Name of God," 27.

Love is the connecting virtue. In Paul's letters, love is often connected with faith and hope, with love serving as the zenith of virtues. Romans 5 indicates that faith justifies through grace, that character produces hope, and that God's love is poured into our hearts through the Holy Spirit. Galatians 5 claims that love works through faith, and this is all that matters. First Thessalonians 5:8 includes the trio of faith, hope, and love in the believer's armor, and Colossians 1:4–5 names the three in a summary of Christian virtues. Titus 2 exhorts elders to be sound in faith, love, and endurance—connecting endurance later with hope.[30] Finally, 1 Corinthians 13—perhaps the greatest chapter in Scripture addressing unity in the church—describes love as the greatest virtue of all. In fact, one who does not have love ceases to be.

In *Exclusion and Embrace*, Miroslav Volf writes about love as it works within communities where differences have divided them. Love is a giving over of the self to another, as well as receiving the other into the self. Volf's text utilizes the theme of embrace as it represents God's arms outstretched toward humanity. Embracing one another is, in Volf's words, "the Paschal mystery lived out in the world."[31] The act of an embrace opens up space, making room for others. Love, in other words, both gives of oneself and receives from another, constituting a cycle of embrace, mutuality, and Christlike interdependence.

Love is many things, and it has varied and deep expressions, but perhaps one of the most significant is this: love covers a multitude of sins. This phrase hints at forgiveness as crucial to love, but it is also more. It is a Christlike exchange of self and an embrace willing to take in not only the good gifts that persons offer each other but also the sins of the other. Love "covering" sin is an act of incorporation and embrace—over exclusion and blame—and demonstrates full acceptance of the other's imperfect humanity. Love, in other words, encompasses the courage to identify with the shortcomings and wrongdoings of another and attaches to another not only through that which is worthy of love, but also that which is not. In this way, love is the most mature of the virtues.

Finally, love is that power through which the church lives between love of God and love of neighbor, and hence Christian charity extends through mission. *The Catechism of the Catholic Church* summarizes charity in the context of the third article of the creed and the mission of the church.

30. See also the connection between endurance and hope in Romans 5:3–4.
31. Volf, *Exclusion and Embrace*, 131.

Charity is the "soul of the apostolate," the bond of perfect harmony, an interior gift from the Holy Spirit, the soul of holiness, and the means of all sanctification.[32] Charity, in other words, brings together faith and hope in a way that the community of faith *becomes* the power of Christ in the world. Charity sends the apostolate into the world to work with Christ on behalf of God's kingdom. It is truly a labor of love.

Conclusion

This chapter raises the question of what parents, pastors, and congregations hope for the children in their midst. MacIntyre's model of excellent social practices challenges the idea that children who sit still and listen quietly model "good" worship. While behaviors may impede or enhance the practice of worship, the meaning of "good" behavior simply must be reframed if we are to grow as worshipers who seek unity in Christ's body. We argued that worship is a social practice whose excellence is achieved through the goods of glorification of God and sanctification of humanity. The implication is that worshipers who are truly receptive to glorification and sanctification open the door to new ways of responding to children in their midst. Thus, for children and adults alike, we do not seek *good* worship—good music, good behavior, good words—but *excellent* worship imbued with true and thick descriptions of God and God's redemptive story that build up a community's faith, hope, and charity toward God and one another.

Reconsider the child at the beginning of this chapter who was making faces at the people behind him. The act appears disruptive at first glance, and the appropriate response might be, "Turn around and sit still!"—that is, if good behavior is the *telos* of worship. Yet rarely do children disrupt simply to engage in disruption. They often have something else in mind, usually getting attention and connecting with others! In this scenario, making faces at people might also emerge from the boy's capacity for love and to be loved as he connects with the new people he sees.

We have argued that the virtues of faith, hope, and love have a variety of forms and contours. Character traits cannot be statically defined, and they are connected with actions. The boy's capacity for love as demonstrated in silly faces appears very different from the adult who demonstrates the capacity for connection through a handshake or an invitation to lunch.

32. *The Catechism of the Catholic Church*, Chapter 3, Article 9, Paragraph 3, sections: 815, 819, 826, 864.

Both, however, have the potential to contribute to the good of welcoming the stranger. When worshipers reconsider the ways that faith, hope, and love are actions and dispositions that support glorification and sanctification, the liturgy opens itself up to transformation. "Shhhh, sit still, and be quiet," become something more akin to charity in the context of children: "The Lord be with you (even when I do not understand or like your behavior)." In this context adults might also notice what else the child needs in order to participate. Perhaps the child is indeed being disruptive and needs a moment outside the service to reset. Maybe he needs a restroom break. Possibly she is tired (from the sleepover the night before) or hungry (because the family was rushed getting out the door). What if instead of following the initial impulse to quiet our children at the first sign of noise or disruption, we instead sought at least to understand the impulse? What if our eyes followed from the comically distorted face of our child to the shy smile of the person behind them and with a wink or a quick wave, the parent joined the child in embracing the stranger in her midst?

This chapter urges parents, worship leaders, and adults to ask themselves, "What are we missing when we 'Shhh' our children?" Such a posture opens the worshiping body to receive the child and the potential that she has for a vocation in worship—a vocation through which she reveals important dimensions of virtue that adults too frequently miss. Such a posture may also open the door to a new liturgy in which the work of the parents in the pew is supported by those planning and leading worship. Finally, such a posture may open us up to the specific ways children embody faith, hope, and love and lead us to become more like the children who Jesus claims are inhabitants of the kingdom of heaven.

Children
Worship
Incorporation
Virtue
Vocation
Vision

5. Vocation

My sisters and brothers, all Christians are called through baptism
to share in Christ's ministry of love and service.[1]

The coming of the Christ Child signifies the advent of a new world. In
his first and only literary work, Friedrich Schleiermacher writes about
the meaning of Christmas through a dialogue of a small gathering of men,
women, and children. The men offer doctrinal views, the women offer storied examples, and the children offer music. Early in the conversation, the
expectant Agnes claims that a mother's love is present even in a newborn
child. The intellectual lawyer, Leonhardt, challenges her with the idea that
love is cultivated and grows in expectation of one's hopes for one's child. In
a fury, Agnes replies, "Do you believe, then, that love is directed to what a
child can be formed into? What can we form, actually? No, love is directed
toward what we believe to be lovely and divine in the child already . . ."[2]

Agnes' rejoinder captures the essence of the present chapter. Adults
have hopes for children, and formation is critical to their faith journey.
However, children also contribute to the body as children. If one agrees
with Agnes—which we do—one understands that the child is something
lovely and divine *already*. In other words, while we hope they grow into a

1. United Methodist Rite of Ordination in Willimon, *Calling & Character*, 28.
2. Schleiermacher, *Christmas Eve Celebration*, 33.

101

future vocation that reflects a mature faith, children have a present vocation for the church specifically as children.

The seasons of the church offer insight into the Christian understanding of vocation. Schleiermacher frames Agnes' revelation in the context of Advent and Christmas. These seasons represent God's incorporating work, as we discussed in chapter 3. With Christmas, the divine becomes human, and God takes on human flesh and form. Advent, the season leading up to Christmas, alerts humanity of this new kind of incorporation. During Advent, Christians wait for the joyous occasion of the birth of revelation, and in this season, Christians are watchful, waiting earnestly for the coming of Christ.

Advent waiting assumes a kind of vocation, namely that of preparing the way for God to dwell among us in our interior lives and our world. *Maranatha*, the Aramaic formula found in Scripture, means "Lord come!" It marks Advent liturgies and expresses a vocation that includes watchful waiting. Waiting is neither passive nor mere acceptance. Rather, the activity of waiting is about preparing, welcoming, and advancing the kingdom of God.

Christians know they live in an intermediate time. Often called "the now and the not yet," this simple yet profound statement delineates the parameters of how the faithful live as active waiters with a present purpose and vocation. We know we are not yet fully incorporated into God's own life, yet we also believe that in the "now" we have some glimpses of what that incorporation is like. The branch of theology called eschatology pursues this question of what it means to live in the "now" that Jesus' incarnation inaugurated while awaiting the promise of full incorporation in the "not yet."

Given that the Christian church is rooted in the trajectory of God's work in creation and humanity, it seems a truism to argue that Christians ought to be comfortable with the dichotomy of living in the now and living toward the not yet. After all, sanctification is ongoing, sin still pervades, and Jesus has not yet come back. But do Christians really believe that "people in progress" are part of the body? Is the primary culture of our congregations one of welcoming the one who does not yet embody the mature disciple? Is the task of worship and Christian education that of forming children for a future life of faith?

Amy Laura Hall suggests that adults often err in worrying about how children will turn out, rather than affirming that "each child, is 'likely to turn out' at the heavenly banquet—in spite of the quite original ways each child is capable of sinning before the age of twelve."[3] The history and future of children ought to be read through the fact that Christ came into the world for our salvation. As such, the significance and possibilities of children's vocation within the church are reflected in the import of the God-Child, as we discussed in chapter 1, and the eschatological reality is that God's kingdom is both now and not yet.

In this chapter, we address the notion of vocation as it applies to children and approach the idea of vocation through the embrace of the now and the not yet. Children are works in progress, to be sure, and are constantly moving toward greater maturity in faith. They require formation and teaching. They also, however, contribute to the mission of the church in the present. Additionally, the worshiping body that overlooks the vocation of children truncates its mission—even forgets that God's kingdom has begun.

We support our claim by arguing that all are invaluable members of the body of Christ. We analyze Paul's notion of membership, particularly as it applies to gifting and worship. This chapter also considers historical ways theologians have addressed vocation in both helpful and hindering ways. These lead to the question of *why* worship is good for children and *how* children contribute to worship. Working from the previous chapter's framework of internal goods of worship and the three theological virtues that support cultivation of those goods, we explore how children embody aspects of the theological virtues, enabling the body to realize more fully faith, hope, and love toward the end of glorification and sanctification.

Children as Members of Christ's Church

In chapter 1, we addressed Paul's recognition of the diversity of gifts within the body as they are offered in worship. In trinitarian fashion, Paul emphasizes the varieties of gifts and services within the one Spirit and Lord (1 Cor 12:4). He goes on to say that a gospel approach to children includes incorporating them deeply into the church's life. Children are God's gift to the church, and reciprocally, they have gifts to offer the people of God.

Paul's description of membership is compelling and fits with the theme of incorporating diversity in unity that we took up in chapter 3. He uses the metaphor of the body of Christ to describe the church and develops

3. Hall, *Conceiving Parenthood*, 394–95.

the metaphor in the context of 1 Corinthians. As Pauline scholar Jeff Crafton notes, Paul introduces membership in the context of a church that is
fighting over questions of superiority and inferiority.[4] Early on in Paul's
letter, the Corinthians use spirituality as leverage to exacerbate divisions
among them. Whether they were arguing over spiritual gifts or devotion
to wisdom, the true reasons for the conflict are rooted in power dynamics,
and the conflicts were many. Paul exhorts the church to focus on unity and
shared life. Love, as 1 Corinthians 13 articulates, constitutes the center of
Christian community and is the result of a body that recognizes the centrality of unity and, simultaneously, diversity.

Paul describes unity as one body constituted by many members, incorporated by one Spirit through one baptism (1 Cor 12:12–13). Bookend-
ing this passage, Paul emphasizes the common good and calls into question
the idea of any single member's purpose as separate from the body's. If one
suffers, all suffer. If one rejoices, all rejoice. The nature of unity is strong
and serves as the framework for meaning and shared experience. Nevertheless, members are not the same, and Paul advocates for diversity within
the community of faith. He writes of one body but notes the distinct hand,
feet, head, and eye. He even claims that one member cannot make a body
(1 Cor 12:19). Diversity within the one body is a definitive characteristic of
membership in Paul's ecclesiology.

In addition, Paul uses the diversity of members to address spiritual gifts
in worship. Though of the same Spirit, individual members are endowed
with a variety of gifts, services, and activities. He exhorts the Corinthians
to respect and utilize the various gifts instead of competing over them or
trying to strive for a gift that is another's. Paul even uses the language of excellence—the language of virtue (*arete*)—to describe the worshiping body
whose members use their gifts for the good of the whole (1 Cor 12:7, 31).
In fact, he introduces the faith, hope, and love motif central to chapter 13
by calling it the "more excellent way" (1 Cor 12:31). The pursuit of unity
and love and the use of spiritual gifts for God's glory constitute the work of
the people.

The use of the body as a metaphor for membership was not uncommon
in the Greco-Roman world. However, Paul's adaptation of the metaphor
was unusual in ways applicable to the topic of children. New Testament
scholar Dale Martin notes that the use of the body metaphor tended to
support the status quo and discourage conflict that challenged social order.

4. Crafton, "Covenant Theology," 2012.

Based on the presence of hierarchy in the physical body (e.g., head over hand), the metaphor's use in Greco-Roman writings reinforced conservative ideology. While Paul picks up the body metaphor, he emphasizes the interdependence of the members and, in fact, problematizes hierarchy.[5] The letter reveals God giving honor to the inferior member, and Paul instructs the Corinthians to treat the less respectable members with greater respect (1 Cor 12:23–24). God has, in fact, arranged the body itself so that honor might be given to the inferior member, in terms of power and status. Paul's argument in 1 Corinthians is complex; however, Martin asserts that three points are clear:

> . . . the usual, conventional attribution of status is more problematic than appears on the surface; the normal connection between status and honor should be questioned; and we must recognize that those who, on the surface, occupy positions of lower status are actually more essential than those of high status and therefore should be accorded more honor.[6]

Paul's decisive teaching on giving greater honor to lesser members occurs in the context of hierarchical Greek and imperial Roman culture, and he concludes that equality in the way members are valued is part of God's design for the church. Paul's care in dealing with "less important" members of the body is both countercultural and emblematic of his ecclesiology based on the full inclusion—even incorporation—of each member.

Additionally, Paul's ecclesiology initiates the church on the somewhat new path of unity in difference. Martin writes, "The microcosm of the body was used to explain how unity can exist in diversity within the macrocosm of society."[7] Recognizing, respecting, and honoring difference—especially when difference is perceived through the lens of status and power—marks the unified body and reveals the incorporating activity of God's Spirit. Paul's ecclesiology, thus, instructs us that children are to be honored and respected as equally valued members of the body.

The incorporation of children into membership necessitates the incorporation of children in worship, and herein lies a distinguishing aspect of children's vocations—the realm of worship. In 1 Corinthians 14, Paul discusses the excellent use of spiritual gifts for building up the church. In worship, the unity of the body necessitates the participation of each part.

5. Martin, "Tongues of Angels," 564–67.

6. Ibid., 568.

7. Ibid., 563.

Each participates by using one's gifts for the common good. Indeed, God's presence in worship is known when all participate. Paul writes, "When you come together, each one has a hymn, a lesson, a revelation, a tongue, or an interpretation. Let all things be done for building up" (1 Cor 14:26b). As we noted in chapter 1, Beverly Roberts Gaventa's work on Paul and children insists on the important roles that children have and the gifts they bring to worship.[8] Her assertions are based on an ecclesiology in which membership through baptism forms the basis from which all persons offer love and service to God's church.

Vocation of the Child

While one might point to shortcomings regarding the ways children have been excluded or neglected in the church from Paul to the present, the theology of children in the church's history is consistently pro-child and attentive to the notions that Paul raises about the body. Clearly children do not have power, and they warrant special care and attention. Attention to children articulates the importance of their spiritual formation and catechesis, in the need to care for the most vulnerable by way of offering food and shelter, and, more abstractly, in using "child" as a category theologically—particularly in baptismal identity. But what does this mean in terms of children's vocations within the community of faith?

Many theologians throughout the church's history elevated children and their place in the life of the church. Clement of Alexandria believed that the child's truthfulness and lack of concern for worldly affairs was a model for adults to understand their faith.[9] Ignatius of Antioch, Clement of Rome, and Polycarp wrote about ways that children are oriented toward the good. In contrast to pagan views that saw children as dispensable (especially females and sickly ones), early apologists argued that Christians saw children as gifts from God and evidence of a good Creator.[10] John Chrysostom maintained that Christian virtues were available to everyone, not only monks, and that children in particular were exemplary in many aspects of living. Particularly notable in Chrysostom's work is the inclusion of females and girls in his examples.[11]

8. Gaventa, "Finding a Place for Children," 246.

9. Bakke, *When Children Became People*, 59.

10. Ibid., 67–68. This includes Aristides of Athens in particular.

11. Berryman, *Children and the Theologians*, 50.

From the Reformation forward, theologians writing about children actually *live* with children and the tone noticeably shifts. Luther placed emphasis on the formation of children. Horace Bushnell enjoyed playing with children, and he believed they knew a higher kind of play essential for the Christian journey. Unlike Jonathan Edward who sought to convert and baptize children, Bushnell believed that formation and participation were key to life in Christ.[12] Using the Lamentations 4:3 imagery of the ostrich, he coined the term "ostrich nurture" (based on the ostrich's practice of laying its eggs, and then burying and abandoning them) to describe the lack of attention given to the overall formation and participation of children.

Friedrich Schleiermacher lost his son at the age of nine, and when friends tried to comfort him by saying his son was too young to be corrupted, Schleiermacher rejected this. He had already seen the power of Christ's love in transforming even a nine-year-old boy into someone more Christlike. Schleiermacher believed that children were a means of grace. His mother raised him with an emphasis on the importance of play as a way to nurture religious feeling. Children connect with one another through play, he argued, and because Christianity is about relationships, children model that important aspect of the faith. Further, Schleiermacher thought children's sense of aesthetics and their natural intelligence contrasted and supplemented that of adults.

Finally, Jesuit priest Karl Rahner, who also loved children, discussed the child's openness to the idea of eternity. He wrote that children embody

> a state in which we are open to expect the unexpected, to commit ourselves to the incalculable, a state which endows us with the power still to be able to play, to recognize that the powers presiding over existence are greater than our own designs, and to submit to their control as our deepest good.[13]

Some theologians, as we have noted, thought that childhood was a time of preparation for the adult life of faith. However, many believed that children had something significant to offer the church in their current state as children.

There are, of course, many other voices that have addressed the vital place of children in the life of the church. It was not until recently that the writings of women theologians came into the picture. Two thinkers are

---

12. Ibid., 151. See also Bushnell, *Christian Nurture*.

13. Rahner in Marty, *The Mystery of the Child*, 112.

noteworthy in the way they deal with the importance of the child's vocation in the now.

Marcia Bunge expands the church's understanding of vocation. Moving from the traditional definition of vocation as paid work, ordained ministry, or personal fulfillment, Bunge describes Christian vocation as "the notion that God is calling us to a life centered in Christ and to ways in which we meaningfully participate in and contribute to God's work in the world."[14] Children are, appropriately, included in this definition. Bunge connects her theology with the doctrine of the priesthood of believers developed in the Reformation. While this doctrine is applied to the common call of all Christians, Bunge scolds theologians for tending to treat children as "'beneath' the work of serious scholars and theologians."[15]

Bunge examines Luther's theology of the priesthood of all believers with a particular emphasis on children and identifies eight theological dimensions of children's vocation. Three are particularly useful in the context of Christian worship. First, Bunge argues that children's vocation includes learning about and practicing the faith.[16] The implication is that in order to learn about God, one must practice faith through such activities as studying Scripture, praying, praising, and worshiping. While she names worship separately, each of the preceding activities is germane to worship as well.

Second, Bunge refers to biblical passages that call children to teach adults and to act as models of faithfulness. She asserts that especially in the Gospels, Jesus recognizes children's positive influence. To adults, Jesus models openness to the insights of children, and he assumes they have something to offer. Finally, and most importantly, Bunge concludes her list with the aspects of play and presence. She writes, "[A]lthough children are to cultivate their gifts and talents to serve others in the future, at the same time, they have a role of strengthening and enlivening families and communities here and now simply through their openness, playfulness, and ability to laugh and be in the present."[17] She bases her argument in Scripture's understanding of children as gifts, and, like Agnes earlier in this chapter, she urges parents and adults to be thankful for them as they are *now*.

Similarly, Bonnie Miller-McLemore also treats the vocation of the child in terms of what the child offers in the present. While her focus is

14. Bunge, "The Vocation of the Child," 32.

15. Ibid., 33.

16. Ibid., 46.

17. Ibid., 47–49.

on the household, she establishes her theology of vocation in baptism, as it makes children equal inheritors of Christian vocation.[18] The theology of the priestly vocation established in baptism is powerful and connects the themes of children, membership, and vocation. As we noted in chapter 2, baptism is the sacrament of initiation, and whether one's tradition baptizes infants or believers, the Christian vocation can be seen either as a response to or a preparation for baptism. Miller-McLemore concludes her article with an emphasis on children's contributions as they are values in themselves, not merely as a means to a future end.[19]

Theologian Geoffrey Wainwright goes so far as to claim that baptism lays a missionary obligation on a person.[20] In conversation with Anglican J. G. Davies, Wainwright argues that baptism initiates persons into the *missio Dei,* and the baptized person is hence called to pattern his or her life after Christ's. Just as the Holy Spirit anointed Christ, the Spirit is also given over to Christians "in order that they may bear witness in the mission of God to the world."[21]

The problem, Wainwright continues, is that many of the baptized do not actually live into their baptism. Millions of baptized persons "have not the faintest existential notion of the worship, fellowship, service and mission involved in the Christian life."[22] While Wainwright's language is strong, his point is valid; especially in the case of paedo-baptisms, the primary reason that baptized persons do not live out their baptisms is that they do not *practice* the vocation of the Christian in concrete ways. They are not part of the Eucharistic communion, they do not regularly worship, and they are not actively engaged in Christian fellowship. Whether their participation as children was limited or whether they left on their own, the reality of vocation for many of the baptized never takes root. In virtue language, vocation has not been cultivated over time through habit.

If baptism and vocation are truly related, then baptized children who are initiated into Christian community have a role to play. They have work to do that is appropriate to the calling of a baptized Christian or child of

18. Miller-McLemore, "Children, Chores, and Vocation," 316. In this section she interacts with Timothy Wengert, who writes that Luther's connection of baptism with the priestly vocation has this effect: "In one stroke, childhood had become a holy order!" ("Luther on Children," 186).

19. Miller-McLemore, "Children, Chores, and Vocation," 323.

20. Wainwright, *Christian Initiation,* 72.

21. Ibid. Wainwright interacts with Davies' book *Worship and Mission.*

22. Ibid.

God. While Christian vocation intersects with a variety of spheres, as Miller-McLemore suggests, worship is the primary distinguishing practice of the church, and moreover, worship is a fitting place for the child to practice his or her vocation. We now turn to a discussion of the virtues in worship and the particular ways that children practice virtues, contributing to the ends of worship.

Children and Virtue

I (Michelle) started teaching my children the Apostles' Creed and Lord's Prayer as soon as they learned to talk. Our nightly ritual went as follows: I would say a phrase, and they would insert the next word or two. Our church used both frequently in worship, and learning the Creed and Prayer provided an opportunity for them to participate or at least hear familiar words. We had other nightly rituals, including singing hymns or doing a roll call of saints to teach them about the faithful people who preceded us. On occasion Hannah and Johannes learned enthusiastically. More often, they were distracted. Other times, they complained or even refused. In spite of their mixed responses, my husband and I generally persisted, in an effort to habituate both them and ourselves.

Johannes was two years old when we began this ritual. Around that time, I lost a dear friend and mentor, Burton Nelson. I grieved for months, and as I was just beginning my teaching career at the seminary where he had taught, his absence was difficult. About six months after his death, Johannes and I were working on the creed before bed. Our exchange went as follows:

> Me: I believe in God . . .
> Johannes: The Father almighty.
> Me: Maker of . . .
> Johannes: Heaven and earth.
> And so on. We continued to the third article.
> Me: I believe in the . . .
> Johannes: Holy Spirit,
> Me: the holy catholic . . .
> Johannes: Church,
> Me: the communion of . . .
> Johannes: Burton.

We stopped. I was surprised and moved. I do not know why he thought of it then, but he inserted the name of my dear friend in the right place, in the right way, and at the right time. Eight years later, I still remember the rich way my son embodied faith, hope, and love—by speaking a single word.

The only way he could have made the appropriate substitution was through his habit of faithful learning. Even when he was distracted, my son acted as though obedience and good habits would lead to something good. Faith was related to his trust and to his surprising application of a powerful truth. He also exuded hope by reminding me of Burton's association with the saints, incorporating me into the resurrection reality. Finally, he showed love by knowing me and being present. He had never known Burton, but he knew at some level that I had experienced a loss. His attentiveness to my personhood in the midst of an ordinary nightly ritual showed a level of presence that could only be the result of love.

Children contribute to the internal goods of worship by embodying the theological virtues in ways that are particular to childhood. Children access and exemplify aspects of each of the virtues that are neglected or even lost in dominant (adult) expressions of virtues in worship. Perhaps Paul calls the church to honor the inferior and less powerful members not only to include them but because they have something crucial to offer the body as a whole!

Faith

C. S. Lewis's classic book *Prince Caspian* transports the Pevensie children—Peter, Susan, Edmund, and Lucy—back to the enchanted land of Narnia. Because time functions differently in this parallel land, the year that has passed in their native England since their initial adventures in *The Lion, the Witch, and the Wardrobe* was equivalent to more than 1,000 years in Narnia. Aslan, the great Lion who redeemed Narnia from the evil powers of the White Witch and faithfully led the children through great dangers, is nowhere to be found. Unsure of what to do, the children attempt to make their way through the surrounding woods.

In the midst of their day's journey, young Lucy catches a glimpse of Aslan. The lion appears to be leading the children in a different direction than the one the elder children think they ought to be traveling. None of the others actually see Aslan, but one of them—Edmund—believes Lucy because she has proved herself trustworthy in the past. But the party ignores her, plunging ahead and in the process finding themselves hopelessly lost. That night, Lucy is awakened by Aslan. He instructs her to wake her siblings and convince them to follow her. If they do not listen, she should follow him without them. Lucy gives Aslan's ultimatum, and the children begrudgingly follow her lead. As they submit, Aslan reveals himself. One by one, each child's eyes is opened to the Lion who had always been in their midst.

Because Lucy could see Aslan in a way her older siblings could not, she followed him and led her elder siblings to a place where they could not go themselves. Her faith enabled her family to encounter Aslan. Children catch glimpses of God in ways that adults simply do not or cannot. Perhaps adults have grown too old, already accustomed to the expected ways that God works. Perhaps the darkness of the world's despair clouds the mature vision. Whatever the case, were adults to open themselves to the faithfulness of children, they too might encounter anew our mysterious, awesome, and wonderful God—or even simply be reminded that God is present in the midst of everyday life. Incorporating children in worship opens the door for them to lead adults into the presence of God.

Faith, as we noted earlier, is often described as right knowledge or assent to doctrine. This is reflected in the familiar response to the question of when children should begin participating in communion. When the child understands the Paschal mystery, then he or she is ready to partake. Knowing what is happening in communion foregrounds discernment about when children can participate. Behind this response is the assumption that the sacraments are for people who have faith, who not only believe in Jesus Christ but also understand what God did in Christ on the cross.

It is true that understanding who God is and what God has done constitutes important, even critical, aspects of participating in the sacraments. However, assent to doctrine is not the only defining feature of faith. In fact, when assent in the form of understanding the sacraments and the Paschal mystery itself is the primary marker, vital aspects of the virtue of faith are cut off or lost. Imagine asking an eight-year-old if she believes that Father, Son, and Holy Spirit are actually present in worship. Then, ask yourself the same question. Which of you really "faiths"? If you say it could be either, then you have underscored our point.

Using assent as the marker for participation in the sacraments represents one way that worship privileges the dominant group and neglects those voices who are not in power. Privileging assent falls within De La

Torre's critique that the content of virtues is always defined by those in charge. Yet if we take a step back and revisit aspects we discussed in the previous chapter—faith as gift, receptivity, doxology, openness, transformation, and trust—we would be hard pressed to make an argument that the grateful or receptive child ought to be fenced from the Table.

Receptivity as it applies to the virtue of faith is indeed about being receptive to God and not other competing powers, and children have great capacity to embody those characteristics of faith as it connects with the triune God. When she was eight years old, my (Michelle's) daughter once corrected me, saying, "Mamma, you don't *take* communion. You *receive* it!" Indeed, the fundamental character of both faith and communion is gift. The ways children embody receptivity and other less emphasized dimensions of faith are too often overlooked in the pursuit of the correct articulation of the mystery as grounds for sacramental inclusion.

Consider the aspect of faith as trust. Before the teen years, children are developmentally dependent on their parents, and when this dependency develops in a healthy setting, children grow to trust their parents deeply. While this trust may be cultivated into adulthood, the independence that emerges with maturation counteracts the kind of "blind" trust that children have in their caretakers. They trust not because they have some special power to trust—they trust their caretakers because they have to. They have little or no alternative. When this relationship flourishes, the part of trust necessary for survival fades into the background because the trusting relationship is primarily one of love or enjoyment. Most children, even those in abusive situations, want to be with their parents.[23]

Judith Gundry's work on children's objective dependence on God is again pertinent here, for she concludes that the extreme dependence of children foregrounds the promise that children are heirs of the kingdom. The reality of children's dependence is so powerful, in fact, that Scripture uses the child as a trope throughout both Testaments to depict faith as utter trust in God. Children, then, are not only helpful examples of what God is looking for in faith as trust; they are necessary for practicing faith in its fullness.

The capacity to be receptive to grace marks another dimension of faith. Children are as attuned, if not more, to this aspect. When I (Michelle) spoke recently at a camp for young children, I preached on ways the knowledge of

23. For more on this see Roisman and Groh, "Attachment Theory," and Berryman, *Children and the Theologians*.

God fills the earth.[24] I asked them to "receive" this knowledge of God filling the earth through their five senses. Open your eyes and see God. Open your ears and hear God, etc. Throughout the week, children relayed the plentiful ways they had seen, heard, smelled, touched, and tasted God. One saw God during a potentially dangerous tubing incident, remarking that God had protected him. Another heard God waking her up like a chirping bird. Another tasted God's goodness in fresh bread. Each of these faithful expressions combines receptiveness to God with thanksgiving for God's abundant gifts.

The work of religious educator and Hebrew scholar Sofia Cavalletti is devoted to children's formation in the church and the ways that children come to own their faith by learning to participate at early ages. In *The Religious Potential of the Child*, she notes that often Sunday school curriculum focuses on stories or propositional ways of approaching the Christian faith. She argues that many Bible stories, while they may enculturate children or impart correct information, do not actually encourage children to enter the story of God's ongoing work of salvation.[25] A Bible story such as Noah's ark includes enough details that its telling invites passive reception of the information rather than an active engagement with it. As exciting as the tale of Jonah and the whale is, everything is done for the child in the telling of it. The story is told from beginning to end, and it is difficult for the child, or the adult, to find a place in these self-contained stories.

Cavalletti argues that children learn, own, and form baptismal identities by encountering God through active participation. By participating, children learn their place in God's story and are later able to connect with Bible stories and other aspects of the orthodox faith because they are already integrally located in the narrative. Cavalletti suggests using parables such as the Good Shepherd as a paradigm for teaching Christian truths broadly. Children more ably find themselves (perhaps as sheep) in the story and relate to characters (perhaps the Good Shepherd as pastor) in ways they understand. Moreover, parables usually have multiple layers of meaning and offer gaps that children can fill in. Such activity is not making up faith. On the contrary, it is the opening up of oneself to God's word as part

24. The Old Testament professes that glory and knowledge of God fill the earth, e.g., Numbers 14:21–22, Isaiah 11:9, and Habakkuk 2:14. Augustine develops this wonderfully in Book X of the *Confessions*. Jim Bruckner recounts the rich ways God's glory is mediated in creation. See his "A Primer on God's Created Glory."

25. Cavalletti, *The Religious Potential of the Child: Experiencing Scripture*, 5.

of our identity and purposefulness. Such an openness and receptivity to God are vital elements of the virtue of faith.

Finally, faith is about obedience to God. While adults and children alike are called to faithful obedience, the fact is that obedience constitutes a significant aspect of the child's reality. A child's obedience in worship has the potential to draw independent, competent adults into the reality of faith as obedience. This form of obedience is far deeper than simply being quiet in response to a parent's "Shhh," or sitting still in worship. Obedience as it relates to faith points to active participation in honoring God and others and in forming loving relationships. For young children, participation in the form of helping is powerful. They might help change the paraments or cloths in the sanctuary. They might help with baking bread or ushering or, connecting with Miller-McLemore's domestic vocation, setting up or cleaning up after communion. For older children, faithful obedience might take the form of participation in Scripture reading or sitting with younger children and helping them worship. Many creative forms of obedience may occur in worship. Our point is that obedience is linked with glorification and sanctification and is therefore a kind of participation in worship. The child who passes the communion plate and faithfully recites the words, "This is Jesus' body!" reminds the adults that they might do the same as they pass the plate to their brothers and sisters in Christ.

If we define faith as assent, trust, and receptivity, then faith moves us toward glorification of the triune God. We glorify God when we assent to the work of God in our life and our world, when we add our "Yes! Amen!" to the voice of God that sings reconciliation, peace, and love into our world, and when our lives are embodied assents to the vision of the kingdom of God. We glorify God when we trust that the future rests in the hands of a God who is "gracious and compassionate, slow to anger and abounding in steadfast love" (Psalm 145:8). Most obviously, we glorify God when we respond to the work of the triune God in our lives and in our world with doxology, thankful to God, the Giver of all good gifts. Through an assenting, trusting, and praising faith we glorify our God.

Hope

Just as the child in our midst teaches adults about a doxological, receptive, and trusting faithfulness, so the child in the worshiping community embodies the hope that our congregations and world so desperately need. Hope is about time, and time is about Sabbath, and Sabbath is about worship. The Old Testament discusses Sabbath in terms of cycles of time (weekly, yearly, jubilee, etc.). Central to these cycles is the day God rests, celebrating the goodness of the previous days' work. Time is marked by God's presence, and when we are called to Sabbath, we too are called to be present to the goodness of God's blessings in the moment. Sabbath represents an important aspect of hope as it includes celebration and lament, laughter and weeping. In worship, hope is knowing that God's "not yet" sustains the faithful to be actively present in the "now."

Children are masters at real time. Unlike their adult counterparts who can easily spend an entire worship service dwelling on a past wrong or a future anxiety, children have an innate immediacy with the present. This is often why they find it difficult to sit still! From the scenario at the opening of this book recall the child who approaches the table with the simple words, "I'm so thirsty!" and then proceeds to move toward the cup. The child believes that her current need (thirst) will be filled by the future act of drinking from the cup—which the pastor has called "the gift of God for the people of God." It is hope because it combines God's future with the present reality. Moreover, the child who acts on her thirst in the context of the sermon and the communion prayer demonstrates active participation in the present drama, namely worship. Finally, the act itself is the proper posture toward God, another dimension of hope. The enactment of the drama explicitly links the child and those who hear her into God's saving work. Remember that the pastor himself marvels as he receives a new vantage point through the children's responses.

In the context of worship, the ability to find peace in the present allows a person to wholeheartedly glorify God. After all, glorification of God is a "now" activity, and children's ability to be present in the moment draws adults into this dimension of glorification. Presence in the moment also renders worshipers able to receive a word of direction, comfort, or challenge that continues the lifelong process of sanctification. The hope is that thirst leads to the cup, and that the cup draws one into the lifelong work of cooperating with God's Spirit, moment by moment. As Benedictine Sister Joan Chittister notes, "It is we who are trapped in the past, angry at what formed us, or fixated on a future that is free from pain or totally under our control. But God is in our present, waiting for us there."[26] If children can

26. Chittister, *The Rule of Benedict*, 27.

help lead us to the present in worship, they can lead us to a God who is waiting for us there.

This immediacy, however, can be a two-edged sword. Whether through socialization or the ability to delay gratification, many adults can endure even the most tedious of sermons or pastoral prayers. Because children live in the present, however, they expect the present to be worthy of their attention. The child who whispers a bit too loudly, "I'm bored!" or audibly yawns in the middle of the sermon may simply be running on too little sleep. Or, he may be challenging the congregation and pastors to live up to the encounter with the triune God as promised through worship. (He also may be voicing the secret thoughts of many in the congregation!) Fidgeting, whispering, and daydreaming are all signs of an unfulfilled present and a desire to grasp the now from the jaws of wearisome monotony. Perhaps if more of us became like little children and inhabited the present, we would discover God in the present—the God who transforms our empty rites into an encounter with the living God.

The hope that allows a child to be fully present also confers upon the child a posture of openness toward the present and the future. As Karl Rahner notes, "Childhood is openness."[27] Within the life of a child, this openness leads her to believe that anything is possible. Church doors really are portals into another world. Fantastical dreams and worlds lay just around the corner waiting to be discovered. How many adults remember finishing *The Lion, the Witch, and the Wardrobe* as children and journeying into the wardrobe or closet, expecting the back wall to become a portal into an enchanted land? A child's inherent receptivity to the unexpected, unlikely, and impossible can open the worship service and the church to the possibility that the future is not simply "more of the same." The future, rather, is pregnant with possibility and imbued with hope.

Two years ago at a Sunday evening service during Advent, I (Dave) was leading a routine service focusing on the Advent themes of waiting and watching for the appearance of God. After a few hymns and prayers, we opened up an extended time of meditation and prayer. After five minutes of silence, a worship leader stood and led the congregation in prayer, ending it with the Advent refrain, "Come, Lord Jesus." For those of us used to traversing this Advent path, the refrain had been so deeply engrained that it rarely

27. Rahner, "Ideas for a Theology of Childhood," 48. For an overview and analysis of Rahner, see Marty's chapter "Wonder in the Provision of Care," *The Mystery of the Child*, 107–17.

surprised us anymore. A four-year-old girl sitting in the back row with her parents brought the congregation back to the stunning wonder of this accalamation, however. In awe, she whispered loudly, "Jesus is coming here?" We had grown so accustomed to the refrain that we needed a reminder by a child who actually believed the words we prayed and anticipated the future the liturgy professed.

The child's openness can lead the congregation toward a hope that loosens adults' attempts to control the future. The presence and hope-filled possibilities inherent in children can aid adults in inhabiting and embodying a hopeful future in light of the present and coming kingdom of God. Through hope, the church participates in the future rather than submitting to fate. The openness of the child—to which the metaphor of child in Scripture refers—leads worshipers to risk a kind of "human childhood" characterized by an "infinite openness" to the work of God in the present. Openness to possibilities, as shaped by promise and the in-breaking of God's kingdom, is foundational to the virtue of hope.[28]

Finally, through inhabiting the present in a posture of openness toward the future, children lead adults back to the present with new eyes to experience the wonder of the now. Wonder perhaps is the most obvious of children's gifts. Adults may rush past the beauty of the world with their thoughts in the future and their faces in their smart phones. A child is more likely to be entranced by the moving cloud, awed by the solitary leaf, wonderstruck by the night sky. Even the child's incessant questioning—"Why?"—is a sign of the insatiable wonder and curiosity about their world. In his *Apology for Wonder*, philosopher Sam Keen offers an image-laden definition of childhood wonder:

> Wonder, in the child, is the capacity for sustained and continued delight, marvel, amazement, and enjoyment. It is the capacity of the child to approach the world as if it were a smorgasbord of potential delights, waiting to be tasted. It is the sense of freshness, anticipation, and openness that rules the life of a healthy child. The world is a surprise party, planned just for me, and my one vocation in life is to enjoy it to the fullest—such is the implicit creed of the wondering child. Reality is a gift, a delight, a surprise—in fact, a toy; it is an excessive, superabundant cafeteria of delights, and should any experience begin to be jaded by boredom and staleness, all one has to do is move on to the next. To wonder is to

28. Marty, *The Mystery of the Child*, 48.

live in the world of novelty rather than law, of delight rather than
obligation, and of the present rather than the future.[29]

How would the worship life of faithful communities be transformed were
they infused with Keen's description of childlike wonder? Imagine a church
who is more motivated by the Spirit of adaptability than the letter of the
law. Consider a church whose experience of worship is delight rather than
obligation. Picture a church that neither rests on the laurels of a storied
past nor anxiously awaits a fearful future. By helping adults experience the
present as an overabundant gift, wonder not only transfigures the moment
but shines its light of delight, marvel, amazement, and enjoyment into the
unknown darkness of the future. In short, wonder endows people with the
courage to hope. Thus, when we enter a worship service laden with guilt
from our past or worries about the unknown, perhaps we must look to the
child and follow her hopeful lead into the presence of the triune God.

If faith leads to glorification, it is in hope that we travel the road of
sanctification. At first blush it may seem that hope and sanctity have little
to do with one another. Sanctity seems much more about the discipline
of living a pious life, while hope is an openness to the wonder that leads
to a positive transformation of the future. Hope seems like an eternal gift,
while sanctification strikes us as an unending task. Perhaps this is because
we tend to view sanctification as endless behavior modification and joy-
less obedience to a list of theistic rules and regulations. Yet sanctification
is not about the act of stripping ourselves of petty sins and vices but rather
about being transformed into the likeness of citizens of the kingdom of
God. Hope gives us the vision of the kingdom of God; sanctification is the
individual and corporate response. Our final hope, our ultimate *telos,* is the
kingdom of God. And when we catch a glimpse of this future hope, our
present lives and actions are transformed in the light of this purpose.

This transformation is sanctification. If Jesus was serious in his assertion that the kingdom of God belongs to those who are like children, then
sanctification is the process of replanting ourselves in the present, resisting
the narrowing parameters of cynicism, and recovering the child of wonder that God created within us. As Rahner notes, "In the child a person
begins who must undergo the 'wonderful adventure of remaining a child
forever.'"[30] Sanctification is that wonderful adventure.

29. Keen, *Apology for Wonder,* 104.
30. Rahner, "Ideas for a Theology of Childhood," 50.

Charity

"A mother's love . . . is what is eternal in us," says Agnes to Leonhardt in the middle of their Christmas Eve argument.[31] Phrased in this way, Agnes' meaning is not exactly clear. Does the eternal about which she speaks reside in the giver or the recipient of love? Likely, it lies in the idea that love happens between people. It is both unifying and relational, and it mirrors the eternal.

Love is the virtue that supports all other virtues and as such is the most perfect and most mature. In many ways, the virtue of love in the way we have described it is more readily noticeable in the capacities of adults than children. For example, parents' depth of love for their children noticeably takes on the qualities of hoping all things, bearing all things. It is patient, kind, and even willing to accept the other in her brokenness and sin. Love is God's gift, but the demonstration of strong parental love draws one very close to understanding the depth of God's love for humanity.

Children also demonstrate the Corinthian aspects of love in pronounced ways. For example, love endures all things, and it is patient. In the context of worship, the culture and expression is predominantly, if not exclusively, the culture of adults. Our scenario of the Church of All Creatures Great and Small at the beginning of the book strikes such a strange chord precisely because children directing the flow of worship is unheard of! The ability of children and youth to be present in most worship services stems largely from their capacity to show charity. The unity they demonstrate, even when they do not understand what adult worship is all about, is remarkable and connects deeply with Paul's view of patience in the body.

Children have much to contribute to the virtue of charity as it expresses the glorification of God and the sanctification of humanity. In the close of chapter 4, we discussed charity as the virtue that, among other things, moves the community more deeply into God's life (and by extension, into one another's). When Johannes inserted Burton's name into the Apostles' Creed, he lovingly moved the recipient (Michelle) more deeply into God's life, and by extension, into Johannes' own life as well as Burton's. While all three virtues have strong communal dimensions, charity most intimately expresses the community of the Godhead. As such, charity must develop and find expression moving humanity, or more specifically

31. Schleiermacher, *Christmas Eve Celebration*, 33.

the body of Christ, toward God in worship. In this fundamental aspect of charity's expression, children are crucial players.

Charity is about unity. Sofia Cavalletti posits the presence of a mysterious reality in a union between God and the child.[32] She offers numerous descriptions of religious experiences of children, arguing that they are complex and deeply existential, in many cases prior to indoctrination. In one instance, she relays a conversation in which a five-year-old child asks his mother whether she loves him or God more. When the mother says "him," meaning the child, the child retorts, "I think this is your big mistake."[33] At some level, the child accepts the idea that humans are made to love God first and foremost. With children, though these moments tend to be glimpses rather than sustained ways of being, interior attitudes constitute an important aspect of their development and what they communicate (verbally and behaviorally).

Charity is also about relationship, and in this regard, the activity of play points to inviting ways that children form relationships. Children play. It is what they do all the time, and their play constitutes the grounds for development, learning, and connection. In his well-known work on godly play, Jerome Berryman notes that children's play prepares them to participate in ways that encourage creativity within the boundedness of the "worship" game. He discusses the ways that worship promotes thinking about God rather than entering into the experience of God.[34] While both are important, thinking rather than feeling tends to dominate. Lack of one or the other impedes relationship growth, and hence charity. Berryman notes that children tend toward feeling, and they creatively express this proclivity through play.

Play not only allows them to invest in the moment, it also serves as the parameters by which to participate and to connect with other players. In the introduction to *The Sacred Play of Children*, liturgist G. Thomas Ryan makes a distinction between religious education and sacred play. Sacred play, he notes, is the activity of praising, singing, and praying—among other liturgical acts—oneself into one's place in the Lord.[35] Prayer, in particular, forms a relationship with God.

32. Cavalletti, *The Religious Potential of the Child: Experiencing Scripture*, 32.
33. Ibid., 35.
34. Berryman, *Godly Play*, 97.
35. Ryan, *The Sacred Play of Children*, x.

The idea of sacred play and performance endows worship with a sense of connection and relationship. Worship professor Todd Johnson and theater professor Dale Savidge develop worship and play in the context of the theater experience.[36] They note that active participation in the theater is like worship. Both are incarnational and involve a sense of relatedness or community. Like worship, the play also occurs in shared space and time. Moreover, the relational and uniting activity of play comes starkly to the fore when one considers the contrast—the virtual world.[37] Thus, worship involving play—as incarnational and sharing space—directs the congregation toward charity through relationship.

Catholic priest Romano Guardini has a similar argument in terms of children's participation in the liturgy. He argues that liturgy exists not for the sake of humanity but for God. In liturgy, worshipers direct themselves to God, and good liturgy moves individuals and congregations from self-consciousness to being present in God. In this way, Guardini regards the liturgy as play. Children play for the sake of play, not for another purpose. He calls play "life, pouring itself forth without an aim, seizing upon riches from its own abundant store, significant through the fact of its existence."[38] He also goes so far as to say that an overly didactic liturgy "denaturizes" worship, causing it to lose its life.

Charity, unity, and relationship are about connecting with one another in shared activity. When my (Michelle's), introverted daughter was young, my husband and I noticed that adults struggled to connect with her. This was not for lack of effort, but rather because they tended to relate to her as a little adult. In other words, they simply tried to talk to her. My husband, who happens to be very good with children, would tell them, "The only way to get Hannah to befriend you is to play with her." Playfulness is not merely the joyful activity of children—it is the forging of love and relationship, the very content of the gospel.

In terms of moving us along the path of glorification and sanctification, love is the ground of faith and hope, the path and destination. Love is sinew that binds together the body of Christ and allows us to make the difficult communal journey toward glorification and sanctification. First Corinthians 13 makes clear that without love, faith and hope are worthless. We cannot truly glorify God or undergo sanctification without being awash

36. Johnson and Savidge, *Performing the Sacred.*

37. Ibid., 119.

38. Guardini, "Retrieving the Tradition," 111.

in the river of God's love, allowing that love to flow out of us and mediate all our relationships. With love we can truly be incorporated into the triune life of God, for "God is love" and "everyone who loves is born of God and knows God" (1 John 4:7–8). Firmly rooted in the love of God, we can faithfully glorify God and hopefully enter a life of sanctification until we enter the kingdom of Love with all of the children of God.

Conclusion

The biblical and sacramental witness of the church calls us to reexamine the vocation of children in our liturgical life. Children and adults have the potential to benefit each other mutually in the activity of corporate worship. Children are given models to follow and a story to inhabit that helps them construct and grow into the meaning of faith. On the other hand, the entire congregation witnesses the unique ways in which children embody the theological virtues of faith, hope, and love that propel the congregation toward the glorification of the triune God and sanctification of the body. Children often hear the gospel with awe, mystery, and delight, invoking the joyful four-year-old's exuberant response: "Jesus is coming here!"

The four-year-old's words signal the eschatological kingdom moving from Advent to Christmas, from the now to the not yet. Both require vocations that advance God's kingdom. When the adults in Schleiermacher's *Christmas Eve* decide to get serious about their discussion, the first topic is music. The banter becomes focused, and the earlier mood of the festivities flattens. The men seem to focus on the "not yet." The women emphasize the "now." In the midst of it all, the child Sofie finds her vocation—she *plays* music, and inserts herself into the center of the adult world. Though the reader may be aware of Sofie's contribution to the unfolding of Christmas, the adults are not. Schleiermacher does not make the in-breaking of the child explicit until the very end, when a late guest, Josef, arrives with a word.

> For me, all forms are too rigid, all speech making too tedious and cold. Itself unbounded by speech, the subject of Christmas claims, indeed creates in me a speechless joy, and I cannot but laugh and exult like a child. Today all human beings are children to me, and are all the dearer to me on that account. The solemn wrinkles are for once smoothed away; the years and cares do not stand written on the brow. Eyes sparkle and dance again, the sign of a beautiful

and serene existence within. To my good fortune, I too have become just like a child again. . . . I feel at home, as if born anew into the better world. . . . Come, then, and above all bring the child [Sofie], if she is not yet asleep, and let me see your glories, and let us be glad and sing something religious and joyful![39]

Josef opens himself up not only to the good news of the child in his midst but also to the way Sofie incorporates him into the present and coming kingdom. While everyone else banters about the meaning of Christmas, Sofie and Josef worship their way into God's glory.

---

39. Schleiermacher, *Christmas Eve Celebration*, 86–87.

Children
Worship
Incorporation
Virtue
Vocation
Vision

6. Vision

Incorporating difference in worship is a risk that invites what J. R. R. Tolkien calls a *eucatastrophe*. Tolkien's invented word literally means "good disaster." A eucatastrophe is an impending catastrophe that ends not in the expected destruction but in a sudden, joyous, and redeeming turn.[1] The turn is not an escape, but rather a miraculous grace that none can predict or concoct. It presumes the possibility of sorrow and even failure as it gives way to deliverance. Tolkien writes,

> It does not deny the existence of dyscatastrophe, of sorrow and failure: the possibility of these is necessary to the joy of deliverance; it denies (in the face of much evidence, if you will) universal final defeat and in so far is evangelium, giving a fleeting glimpse of Joy, Joy beyond the walls of the world, poignant as grief.[2]

Eucatastrophes risk unpredictable outcomes for the sake of new worlds.

Anything that upsets the status quo can lead to a holy mess. Shifting control invites uncertainty. Ceding power begs variability. Incorporating otherness can provoke fear and possibly incite chaos. What if the worshiping body were to reconsider these risks as potential for eucatastrophes? The roots of eucatastrophe, "good destruction" or "good disaster," are pregnant with possibility. The concept urges congregations to consider which

1. Tolkien, "On Fairy Stories," 13–14.
2. Ibid.

ideas and habits may need to be destroyed in order to open the way for *evangelium*.

We affirm the care and integrity that goes into planning a worship service, and we applaud preparation or leadership. Yet amidst planning and executing worship, leaders must open themselves up to the differences, even the radical otherness, in their congregations. Incorporation risks failure, even spectacular failure. Yet leaders and congregations who open themselves up to good destruction make room for sudden turns and God's miraculous grace.

We have spent the preceding chapters building the argument toward the vocation of children in worship. We emphasize marks in relation to God's kingdom essentially because our vocation in worship extends beyond the church and into the world. In this final chapter, we envision the implications of the child fully incorporated in worship as that worship extends into the world and transforms God's people in ongoing ways. We conclude that the habits of incorporating children in worship make way for a communion to incorporate other even more threatening kinds of difference such as ethnic, cultural, and gender differences.

No Children Allowed: Tolerable Unity

The manner in which the Israelites treated their children, especially the most vulnerable, reflected the state of Israel's relationship with Yahweh. In other words, it was not *only* about the children. If they treated the orphan unjustly, it was a symptom that the Israelites were straying from the commandments of God and not living up to their side of the covenant. The Old Testament diagnoses the symptom of not caring for the vulnerable quite simply—when they are not faithful to God, they are not faithful to one another.

Israel's neglect of the vulnerable was accompanied by idol worship. Old Testament scholar M. Daniel Carroll argues that the prophets admonished the Israelites because they bifurcated social justice and worship. He writes that in the Old Testament, "Much is at stake in the community's worship." Good worship questions reigning ideologies, engages harsh realities of life, and nurtures a commitment to God's justice.[3] An integral connection exists between the excellent worship of God and the ethical lives of God's people.

3. Carroll, "Can the Prophets Shed Light," 216–24. For more on this, see Carroll, "Seeking the Virtues."

Just as the mistreatment of children signified disunity in the nation of Israel, so too the absence of children in our worship represents the disunity in our congregations. This disunity has many causes. It may indicate a theology of the church that is only comfortable with unity as sameness. As mentioned in chapter 1, this is inclusion without regard for differentiation and difference. It is merely a tolerable unity.

Moving beyond such so-called unity is difficult. My (Michelle's) grandfather shed many tears over a man named John. When my grandpa was an elder, John started coming to his church. John dressed in jeans and old shirts, and was not as put together as the regular attenders. Because my grandfather was a longtime member—both well-respected and kind—leaders in his church urged him to tell John that it was not appropriate to come to church dressed as he did. Would he please clean up and put on a suit? Hesitantly, my grandpa did their bidding and relayed the church's sentiments to John.

John never came back. Two weeks later, when my grandfather tried to contact John, he learned that John had committed suicide. My grandfather wept. Up until the day he died at age 91, he lived with the pain of his actions. He should have gotten to know John. He should have conveyed his hesitancy to the other leaders. He should have noticed that no one really talked to John. My grandfather cried because he believed that had he welcomed John into the congregation as he was, perhaps John would have glimpsed the unqualified love of Christ.

John's death was not my grandfather's fault. My grandfather belonged to a church who wanted people who were different to become just like them. This was a congregation that had yet to understand faithful incorporation in all of its accompanying brokenness, messiness, and chaos. Even those with the best intentions could not see the other for the difference he offered. They wanted a tolerable unity.

The most common theological error is to misplace the focus of worship from God to a group of people or an individual. The tendency is to ask what one gets out of worship rather than what one brings to worship. Otherness becomes a barrier to the dominant group getting what it wants out of worship: predictability, spiritual fulfillment, preferred music, etc. The dominant group shapes worship in its own image, eliminating what it deems to be unnecessary, unappealing, intolerable, or different.

Incorporating otherness, beginning with children, opens congregations to consider what may need to be destroyed—even (or especially) when it comes to tolerable unity. Perhaps the unity lies in a professionalism that appears impressive but does not allow another's less polished gifts to be cultivated. Or perhaps it lies in the pastor's charisma that brings excitement but does not allow for active participation from others. Perhaps the unity lies in an entrenched order that offers stability but does not allow for the spontaneity of those who may not understand the order. Each of these kinds of unities has the potential to contribute to good worship, but if the body does not welcome otherness, its unity is merely tolerable.

Consider the child-induced catastrophe in the Gospel of Matthew as it breaks through the unity confined to the Pharisees' way of doing things. Jesus enters the city to the cries of "Hosanna to the Son of David!" and then continues toward the temple where he drives out the moneychangers and the shopkeepers. He takes up residence in the temple, healing the sick and the lame. Children descend, gathering at the temple and crying out of turn: "Hosanna to the Son of David!"

The Pharisees, no doubt infuriated by the lack of protocol, angrily question Jesus. "Do you hear what [the children] are saying?" Jesus replies, "Yes; have you never read, 'Out of the mouths of infants and nursing babies you have prepared praise for yourself'?" (Matt 21:15–16). Jesus understood that the children expressed the truth and responded well to his momentous entry. They created a eucastrophe, upsetting the existing social and liturgical order and making way for the *evangelium*. Jesus' rebuke is about more than how children are treated. It is a diagnosis of a kind of uniformity that leaves no room for the love of God and the parallel love of the other. As Jesus rebukes idolatry and disordered sameness, the praise of children opens the way for a joyous turn toward difference that binds faithfulness to God and faithfulness to one another.

Vision of Incorporation: Disruptive Unity

Incorporating those who are different in worship risks reforming the liturgical and ecclesial life of the church toward the end of advancing God's kingdom. The work of incorporation is risky because it requires leaders and laity to cede power and to radically open themselves up to the other. Any time we engage those who are normally muted or excluded and welcome the participation of new groups, power shifts. When worshipers commit to more than a tolerable unity, they invite sorrow and failure, but they also open themselves to the possibility of deliverance.

Thus, incorporation engenders the virtue of courage on the part of the liturgical leadership and the worshiping body. Courage does not mean the fear of risk disappears. It means groups or persons act for God's goodness or justice despite their fear. Humans fear difference and even see difference as a threat. The other can represent people of different social classes, ethnicities, sexual orientations, political affinities, or ages. Rather than viewing incorporation of the other(s) as a means to represent the diverse kingdom of God, groups learn to fear change and the loss of the status quo that accompanies it. Yet ceding power and being radically open to the other are dimensions of Christian worship and Christ's own model of incorporation. Christ—the great other—ceded divine power to become human for the redemption of the world. His ministry was marked by a risky openness. A courageous congregation follows Christ's model fearfully, learning to risk the right things.

For leaders to give up control of the future can seem the more dangerous aspect in the context of worship. As a liturgist and worship leader who takes the craft of liturgy seriously, I (Dave) find this to be one of the most difficult steps. There are few things more frustrating than spending hours writing and forming the order of worship only to have it mishandled by worshipers or other leaders. Behind this fear is the assumption that *my* craftsmanship draws people into the presence of God. Ceding power and control takes courage to trust that when we are faithful to our vocations in worship—as leaders or as lay people—God and the worshiping community may work outside of our expectations. Such trust requires a robust pneumatology that affirms the Holy Spirit's movement, not simply in the well-ordered and beautiful, but also in the flaws, missteps, and bungling that happens in shared life.

Incorporation also requires courage on the part of the powerless. Incorporation affirms the worth of all and invites those outside the dominant group to claim their place within the church. If welcomed, people are generally eager to accept and execute their vocations in worship with care, knowing that they too are responding to the living God. Even so, it takes courage to claim their rightful inheritance as children of God and full members of Christ's body.

Sharing power builds the kind of communal character that is prepared to act courageously beyond the walls of the church. Consider courage in the context of race and ethnicity. Brian Bantum argues that fidelity to race occurs both in the oppressed, or minority groups, and in the oppressor, or dominant groups. The only hope for a unity that incorporates diversity is for both oppressor and oppressed to submit to transformation. He bases his argument in baptismal identity and calls all Christians to submit their embodied markers to their baptismal identity. Bantum is not suggesting that we ignore the color of our bodies or the ways in which people perceive and react to them. He is suggesting that the baptized live as though transformation of our identities in Christ is possible.[4]

Willie James Jennings calls this kind of baptism disruptive. Disruptive baptism does not solidify one's current identity or weave it "seamlessly into a community." Disruptive baptism opens one's identity to something different. In other words, what we are really baptized into is *multiplicity*, and as Jennings stresses, those who join Christ's body in baptism enter worlds, words, stories, hopes, and dreams that are not their own.[5]

Being open to otherness is not always about the big things, such as worlds and dreams. The small things matter. Bantum, who is biracial, tells his story of marrying a Korean American woman (Gail).[6] Gail likes kimchee; Brian tolerates it. Offering one's identity to baptismal transformation and possibility does not mean that Gail has to transform her tastes and leave her Korean heritage by the wayside—or that Brian must merely put up with it. It means that Brian works from his baptismal identity to be open to Gail's full personhood, including eating kimchee but also including the many other lenses and particular embodied ways in which Gail has been shaped. Her lenses are linked with who he is, and this kind of both/and "mixing" is not about toleration—it is about openness to transformation. Baptism into multiplicity requires both Brian and Gail to submit their identities to each other and to live in hope of their renewal.

As Bantum's story indicates, opening oneself to difference is easier to do with those whom we love and with whom we feel safe, such as spouses or children. Loving relationships can be used as a crutch, or they can become avenues for disruptive unity. Likewise, worship can be used as a crutch, or it can become an avenue for disruptive transformation—a eucatastrophe. It is okay to begin with the small. If we believe that the God we glorify is big enough to sanctify our identities, opening them to the multiplicity and otherness of baptism, then we would do well to open ourselves fully to God's work in small, disruptive ways, beginning with the children in our midst.

4. Bantum, *Redeeming Mulatto*, 182–86.
5. Jennings, "Being Baptized," 285–86.
6. Bantum, "New Birth and the Realities of Race."

Vision of the Liturgy: Improvisation

One can imagine a eucastrophe slipping by without anyone recognizing its potential for grace. One can also imagine a good disaster averted because it was not written in the order of worship. Many in the liturgical reform movement have noted that worship planning tends either toward the comfort of the new or the comfort of the old. The former includes worship services whose order implies that the Spirit cannot work through historic liturgical forms or ancient words. In these churches, worship planning is primarily about being new, distinct, and relevant. The critics of such a perspective no doubt have a point, for Christian worship that is not historic loses much of the diversity of the whole church. Those who exclusively embrace the new may not have the sight, in other words, to recognize the diversity within the historic, universal church.

Yet there is just as much danger on the opposite end of the spectrum. Many high liturgical churches are so well ordered and routinized that they leave little room for improvisation or spontaneity. One could imagine Jesus showing up in a blaze of glory during the Eucharist only to be hushed until the Great Thanksgiving could be completed. The Holy Spirit brings order out of chaos—but the Spirit can also bring disorder when prideful order and uniformity have become the only acceptable way.

In our minds, the best metaphor for this balance that opens a worshiping body to otherness is improvisation, a term most often associated with jazz music.[7] From Louis Armstrong and Duke Ellington to Charlie Parker and Miles Davis, all were masters of improvisation on their particular instrument. Yet what non-jazz musicians often fail to understand is that the seemingly off-the-cuff musical improvisation is grounded firmly in the limits that the chord structure sets on the musician. Each chord change provides a range of notes that the musician can improvise within, but it does provide limits that are honored if one is true to the music and to the other members of the band. Furthermore, musicians improvise successfully by memorizing chord changes and understanding the limits placed upon them. At this level, even a musical mistake can be woven back into the beautiful melody.

So too worship must be ordered yet open, practiced yet fluid, prepared yet poised to go where the Spirit leads. In my (Dave's) own ministry, this has played out in calling forward a person who seems in particular need of

7. For a more detailed analysis of improvisation in the church see Wells, *Improvisation*.

prayer so that the congregation can gather around him, lay hands on him, and intercede with and for him. It has led me (many times!) to change the final hymn of the service because although the one I had originally chosen might have been okay, I realized that another hymn might better witness to the story of God enacted in that place on that particular day. Occasionally, these experiences have also called me to go "off script" during a sermon and speak an unplanned word.

This improvisatory art calls for a mastery of the liturgical elements, a spiritual maturity to discern the difference between an emotional reaction and the still, small voice of the Spirit of God. Improvisation calls for a willingness to make a mistake—to improvise and fail—and illumine the work of God even as it enfolds our mistakes into the faithful melody of God's song. Improvisation teaches us that we must leave room for the unexpected in worship, for when there is no room for the unexpected, there is no room for otherness or for the living God.

As the liturgist clings to control for fear of mistakes, the church often finds itself clinging to homogeneity not through genuine discernment but out of fear. Like an anxious amateur jazz soloist, such a church sticks to the simple notes of the melody rather than ventures off the page and risk playing a wrong note. While this may help avoid mistakes, it creates a monotonous, uninspired song. So too the church that doggedly holds to sameness creates a monotonous, uninspired Christian witness that may be safe but does not resemble the beauty and adventure that marks the Christian story.

Children, adults, and the entire community benefit from learning to improvise. It is vocation of the whole church to participate in being receptive to God's giftings in the body as a whole. Children model trust, openness, receptivity, presence, endurance, and unconditional love. Adults model doctrinal assent, faithful giving, stewardship, and reconciliation. Because the unity is in Christ and not sameness, they have great potential to enact the liturgy in ways that makes room for difference.

Vision of the Kingdom

Good liturgy does not end with children. Incorporation does not end with children. Incorporating children into liturgy invites them into the "work of the people." Systematically extended, the church's habit of incorporation moves into the world as "the liturgy after the liturgy." Thus, incorporation is a habit that births receptivity to other kinds of difference and a communion that more richly reflects the diversity of God's kingdom. The hope is that a people whose unity is in Christ and whose differentiation is in baptism leads the body to take on new worlds.

Mestizo theologian Virgilio Elizondo writes about how those who take on new worlds often live in spaces "in-between." Elizondo upholds Jesus of Galilee as an example who enables people to cross the usual boundaries of power and identity and form a new community. Jesus, as divine, entered into the foreign world of humanity and took on human smallness. The "Galilean principle," as Elizondo calls it, is created out of those tossed aside, such as Christ himself. Elizondo writes, "From the margins, Jesus initiates not a new center but rather a new movement of the Spirit that enables people to cross segregating boundaries and form a new human family based on love of God and love of neighbor."[8] The point of Christian community is not a new center of power, for power is in Christ alone. Christian community is a departure point for new worlds where those who have nothing to offer now have something to offer.

The biblical witness affirms the ways the baptized community takes on new worlds. When the Holy Spirit begins to move in the early church as recorded in the Acts of the Apostles, the disciples are surprised that many Gentiles are not only responding to the gospel message but that they too are being baptized by the Holy Spirit. This raises the fundamental question: how should the Gentiles be incorporated into the covenant relationship with God in the burgeoning church? Should they too be circumcised and follow the same customs (e.g., dietary laws) as the Jews?

To answer this question, the leaders of the new movement gather for the Council of Jerusalem (Acts 15). After debating the issue, Peter and Barnabas stand and give their testimony about how God moved among the Gentiles during their evangelistic mission. Peter speaks:

> My brothers, you know that in the early days God made a choice among you, that I should be the one through whom the Gentiles would hear the message of the good news and become believers. And God, who knows the human heart, testified to them by giving them the Holy Spirit, just as he did to us; and in cleansing their hearts by faith he has made no distinction between them and us. Now therefore why are you putting God to the test by placing on the neck of the disciples a yoke that neither our ancestors nor we have been able to bear? On the contrary, we believe that we

8. Elizondo, "Jesus the Galilean Jew," 277.

will be saved through the grace of the Lord Jesus, just as they will
(Acts 15:7–11).

After further discussion, the council sends a letter to the Gentiles inform-
ing them of their decision: "For it has seemed good to the Holy Spirit and
to us to impose on you no further burden than these essentials: that you
abstain from what has been sacrificed to idols and from blood and from
what is strangled and from fornication. If you keep yourselves from these,
you will do well. Farewell" (Acts 15:28–29).

While the concessions made to the Gentiles are incredibly formative
for the history of the Christian church, the opening line is more important
in our context: "For it has seemed good to the Holy Spirit and to us." Note it
does not say, "We received a voice from the heavens," or "One in our midst
prophesied." Rather, it *seemed* to be the best decision, meaning it could
also have been the wrong one. The council had the courage to listen to the
stories of God's movement in conjunction with the Scriptural witness and
improvise into an uncertain future, ceding their power as Jews and living
"in-between" as the Spirit of God moved in both Jew and Gentile.[9]

The movement in Acts and the work of scholars such as Wells, Bantum, Jennings, Elizondo, and others who engage the idea of taking on new
worlds accentuate the connection between the world of worship and the
world of the kingdom. We now turn to the question of how those worlds intersect. How, in short, do the identity-shaping and habit-forming practices
of worship extend beyond worship to advance God's kingdom?

MacIntyre's definition of a social practice makes clear that the excellences or virtues achieved through a particular social practice are to be
"systematically extended." Recall McIntyre's definition of a social practice as

> . . . any coherent and complex form of socially established coop-
> erative human activity through which goods internal to that form
> of activity are realized in the course of trying to achieve those stan-
> dards of excellence which are appropriate to, and partially defini-
> tive of, that form of activity, with the result that human powers to
> achieve excellence, and human conceptions of the ends and goods
> involved, are systematically extended.[10]

The extension of worship is the missiological component of worship. The
systematic extension of an excellent practice transforms not only the ones

9. This insight and the particular example of Acts 15 comes from Johnson's *Scripture
and Discernment*, 68–80 and 98–106.

10. MacIntyre, *After Virtue*, 187.

engaged in the social practice but also the community, or world, around it. Excellent worshipers, in other words, enrich the world and its narratives outside the church.[11]

If church and world are transformed, you might ask what the difference is between the worshiping community and world it enriches. Those who participate in the social practice of worship excellently are doing so because worship is an end in itself. While an enriched or even transformed world is related to excellent worship, it is not the whole of it. Specifically, glorifying God distinguishes the body of Christ from the world it affects. The goal of excellent worship, then, is not simply to transform the community but *to incorporate the world into the body that glorifies God*. In doing so, the body opens itself up to the sanctifying power of the Holy Spirit. This is why it is missiological. Excellent worship incorporates the world, inviting difference as difference into unity in Christ. Excellent worship extends into new worlds where the faithful incorporate unity and difference as it reflects the triune God.

This idea is the summit of our argument and underscores why children are so important for the church's mission in the world. Missiology is based on a common baptismal vocation. A "broken" fellowship—whose meaning ranges from the body that is inclusive but not diverse to the body that is not inclusive (and not diverse) and everything in between—lacks a united vocation, and its vision, therefore, cannot be one of unity in Christ as it incorporates difference. While children are very much a part of Christianity and the life of the church, they are radically other than adults. Inviting children to participate, engage, and find their voice allows for the cultivation of the theological virtues more richly. Faith, hope, and love make not only for excellent worship, but also for the advancement of God's kingdom. If the virtues are developed more fully by incorporating children into worship, the church develops the courage to be willing to improvise, and even fail, in the attempts to take on new worlds and new kinds of difference.

The church does not reform itself simply for its own good. As the body of Christ, it reforms itself for the sake of its mission. The mission is one of spreading the good news of Christ to the world for the sake of the kingdom. So the church becomes the launch pad from which we are empowered by word and sacrament and propelled into the world to be a foretaste of the

11. By "world" we are referring to the communities that are enriched by the church. We use "world" to avoid the confusion of community referring to the faith community or the local community.

just, loving, and peaceful kingdom of God. The children in our midst can indeed help—even save the church from its grip on power, control, homogeneity, tolerance, and even unity. Children open the body to the uncertain winds of the Holy Spirit that blow where they will, moving the dramatic diversity of God into the certain hope of God's coming kingdom.

Mark of the Kingdom: A Child Shall Lead

The Hebrew word *Sh'cheenah* (Shekinah) means the dwelling place of God. It relates to God's glorious presence with the Israelites and is often associated with consecrated places such as the Tabernacle or the burning bush.[12] Some scholars link the Shekinah and the Holy Spirit. Others link it with the growing manifestation of God in the Word.

Children are also associated with God's Shekinah. Scholars such as Hans-Ruedi Weber maintain that when Jewish leaders and priests went into captivity in the beginning of Lamentations, the Shekinah did not go with them. However, the author of Lamentations hints that when the children went into captivity, God's glory departed with the departure of the children.[13] Weber's assertion taken broadly situates the children in relation to God's glory just as Jesus connects children with God's glory by telling the disciples that the kingdom of heaven belongs to the little children (Matt 19:14). We suffer them, or receive them, because God's kingdom is theirs.

Throughout the book we have shared vignettes from our own congregations in which children's presence, engagement, and voice in worship have built up faith, hope, and love and reflected God's kingdom. Worship that truly incorporates children is imbued with stories, wonder, awe, openness, immediacy, dependency, and trust, among other things. Such worship engenders a community that takes seriously Christ's words that children are a sign of God's kingdom. Congregations that humble themselves before the otherness of children open themselves to other kinds of difference. The vision begins with incorporating children. But it is about more than children. Incorporation adds color and fullness to the grand tapestry of the kingdom of God—a kingdom made up people of all ages from every tongue, tribe, people, and nation, whose eschatological end is worship of the triune God (Rev 7:7–12).

12. See the following examples: Exod 40:34–35, Deut 4:12, 2 Chr 7:2–3, Isa 6:3, Lam 1:5–6, Dan 4:28–32.

13. Weber, *Jesus and the Children*, 28.

The fruits of worship—or the glorification of God—are meant to be shared. The Shekinah moves from tabernacle to kingdom as worship extends into the world. Incorporating children into worship through word and sacrament not only teaches us about the vocation of the Christian life; it forms us in the communion of the triune God and the way of God's kingdom. In this kingdom, children are not new centers of power—they are departure points for new worlds. These new worlds find unity through Christ and common vocation.

New life begins as the smallest of seeds and grows by glorifying God. In this kingdom, even the catastrophe of the crucifixion gives way to the eucatastrophe of the resurrection. In this kingdom, all tears will be wiped away, all mountains laid low, all valleys filled, and all crooked ways made straight. In this kingdom, hope will be fulfilled, faith shall be sight, and only love will remain. In this kingdom, "The wolf shall live with the lamb, the leopard shall lie down with the kid ... and a little child shall lead them" (Isa 11:6). May it be so! Thanks be to God.

Conclusion

It is the fourth Sunday in Advent at the Church of All Creatures Great and Small. A group comprising both young and old gathers around the Advent wreath as the strains of the prelude fade. An elderly woman reads from the prophet Isaiah, and a child carefully lights the Advent candles. It takes two tries and a little help from the children's pastor, but once lit, the wicks signal the burgeoning hope of the promised Messiah to a people waiting in darkness. The wreath is the only light in the worship space. As the candles flicker, one of the lay worship leaders begins the responsive call to worship. Since the congregational refrain is always the same—"Come, Lord Jesus"—nearly everyone can participate, even those whose age, visual impairment, or intellectual abilities prevent them from reading the printed order of service. The expectant faces of the children draw the congregation into the hope that Jesus really is coming.

A guitarist strums as the congregation proclaims the fourth and final refrain of "Come, Lord Jesus" and transitions to the song "All Who Are Thirsty." The verse is a bit difficult for those who cannot read, but the chorus repeats the simple and melodic refrain: "Come, Lord Jesus, come." When the congregation gets to the refrain, all voices join. It is an Advent tradition to sing the same song each week after the call to worship, so individuals and families can accustom themselves to the words. Some have noted singing it prayerfully around their own Advent wreath at the dinner table.

The senior pastor of children and youth leads the congregation. She invites them to join her in a prayer of confession. Using simple words, she articulates a particular area of sin (e.g., "We confess the ways in which we do not treat our neighbor as ourselves."). She makes space for silent confession (even though some of the younger children can be heard wrinkling paper and kicking their feet against the backs of the pews). The pastor concludes with the simple intercession, "Lord, in your mercy." The people respond,

"Forgive us our sins." At that point, many of the fidgeting children look up to listen. The confession continues, moving as a conversation—listen, respond, listen, respond—the systolic and diastolic heartbeat of prayer draws even the youngest into its rhythm. The prayer ends with a prolonged silence that is broken by the joyful words of assurance: "Children of God, believe the good news of the gospel: in Jesus Christ we are forgiven!" A two-year-old claps and squeals—most likely because she notices that (as the pastor has proclaimed the assurance), the string of lights on the Christmas tree is lit to join the light of the Advent candles.

Having been reconciled with God, the congregation reconciles with one another by the passing of the peace of Christ. Soon all are walking to and fro in the sanctuary as young and old share Christ's peace (and perhaps catch up on the goings-on in one another's lives). As the passing of the peace comes to a close, the musicians begin a joyful song of praise as a fitting response to the congregation's twofold reconciliation.

A collegian walks around the sanctuary with a giant canvas bag filled with percussive instruments. He opens the bag to everyone and offers a tambourine or a pair of claves to add rhythm to the song. A three-year-old girl playfully hits her tambourine on the back of her earnest seven-year-old brother, who fiercely concentrates on synchronizing each stroke of the claves with the beat of the song. Their father quickly steps between them so that the little girl may bang on him instead of her brother. When the song comes to a close, the young college man reappears with the canvas bag, and the children, some more reluctantly than others, return their instruments. He has wisely asked one of the more fidgety little boys to help him collect the instruments, and as they finish, the boy guards the instruments in his new seat in the pews as he sits by the young man. The boy's mother appreciates the young man's gesture and enjoys a few minutes of stillness.

A ten-year-old nervously makes his way to the lectern to read Scripture. Although he has practiced with his mom several times, he is anxious. He takes his place at the lectern and looks over the many faces in the congregation. The moisture from his mouth seems to be diverted to his palms. With trepidation and stilted words, the boy begins reading from the prophet Micah. Stumbling over even the most basic words, the boy rushes through the reading, dropping whole phrases in his race to finish. An elderly man bursts out, "Speak up, young man!" The boy's face warms. The only silver lining is the thought of finishing the readings and finding a solitary place in the church basement where he can at least be mortified alone.

As he introduces the Psalter lesson, he chances a look up into the congregation and his eyes fall upon his Sunday school teacher, a seventy-three-year-old woman who has been a member of the congregation since she was his age. What the boy does not know is that his teacher's love and support for children over the years is all the more remarkable given that she herself had lost a child tragically. In spite of her own loss, she offers charity and presence to each child. Far from looking aghast at the mess he had made of holy Writ, she has a serene smile on her face as she gazes up at him. When she catches his eye, she gives him a subtle wink. He steadies himself, takes a deep breath, and begins the responsive Psalm. As the congregation responds to his words, a bit of courage takes hold of him, and his reading becomes more fluid. His knees stop quivering, and his breathing returns to normal. As he finishes with the Gospel lesson from Luke, he speaks with boldness and clarity, proclaiming the good news of the coming kingdom of God. Closing the Bible, he looks up and faithfully announces, "The word of the Lord" as though he believes it. The congregation responds with renewed vitality, "Thanks be to God."

The pastor has progressed through each Sunday in Advent by doing less with words and more with light, and so her homily is short. She declares the good news that Christ not only came to us in the Incarnation but is coming again to establish God's kingdom. Throughout her sermon, she blends story, humor, and biblical insight to weave together a proclamation of the good news that all in her congregation can understand, even if some children and adults find their minds wandering elsewhere.

After the sermon, an offering is collected for the general budget of the church. As the plates are passed around and a middle-aged man sings of the abundant gifts of God, children are invited to come forward and drop their own gifts in a box at the front of the sanctuary. This offering is dedicated to feeding children in the Congo, a place the children learned about in their Sunday school classes. Many children drop coins, while a few proudly display their dollar bill before stuffing it into the box; some walk nervously up to the box, while others run, having clearly anticipated this moment in the service since the call to worship. One child loudly entreats his dad to give him more money so he can make the trip again. When the song finishes, the ushers bring forward the offering plates while the congregation sings "Praise God from Whom All Blessings Flow." Behind the ushers, an older man and a young girl process in with the elements for communion. The girl smiles shyly as she places the bread on the table, skipping back to her parents.

Hands aloft, the pastor leads the congregation in the Great Thanksgiving. Some of the children have memorized their parts, and so the willing ones are able to participate, even though they mumble their way through the difficult parts. The Sunday school teachers have taught the children Isaiah 6:3, and so when the congregation gets to the Sanctus, they join in: "Holy, holy, holy is the Lord of hosts: the whole earth is full of his glory."

The pastor has asked Nicole, a fourteen-year-old freshman in high school, to help serve the bread. While she was anxious about this responsibility, she agreed after a bit of cajoling by her pastor. Taking the bread, she stands next to her pastor who partners with Nicole by taking the cup. Invited to come and taste the grace of God, the people slowly make their way forward as Nichole breaks off large pieces of bread and recites, "The body of Christ, broken for you."

Nicole continues serving, and an elderly man comes forward with his walker. She attempts to reach out and give the man a piece of bread, but the man's unsteadiness causes the bread to fall on the floor. Not knowing what to do, Nichole feels the reassuring hand of her pastor, who whispers, "Move a little closer and give him another piece; don't worry about the bread on the floor." Inching forward, Nicole breaks off another piece of bread, places it securely in the man's hand, and says just above a whisper, "The body of Christ, broken for you." The man nods and shuffles to the cup. The pastor notices that a three-year-old is crawling on the floor, making a break for the lost bread. Hesitating, the pastor looks up at the father, who shrugs and lets the child pick it up and put it in her mouth. As his grandmother whispers a word of reproach, the child's older sister looks up unabashed and protests, "But it's Christ's body, Grandma! You said we were supposed to eat it!" Temporarily speechless, the older woman receives her bread, dips it into the cup, and opens her heart to consider her own obedience.

Standing several people back, Nicole's mother has tears sliding down her face. She is not crying because she is embarrassed or shamed at her daughter's mishap. She is crying because she had been raised in a church where woman were not allowed to serve communion, not allowed to proclaim the Word, and not allowed to teach the older Sunday school classes. She cries tears of joy that her adolescent daughter knows that she is fully God's child, able to share the sacrament with those hungry for it. She has often lamented how adults do not allow children to participate, and she finds healing as she waits for her daughter to serve her.

Even in the mishaps, or perhaps especially in the mishaps, Nicole's mother encounters grace through faith that God is present in Nicole, the elderly man, the scavenging boy, his older sister, and even her own mistakes and missteps. And when she receives the bread from her daughter, dips it in the cup, and places it in her mouth, she is sent back to her pew knowing that this day she has indeed tasted the marvelous grace of the triune God.

The Church of All Creatures Great and Small now lives up to its name. After years seeking to incorporate the great and the small, the members continue to worship. That is all they can do. Some lament that changes are not quick enough. Others take their cue from the children, who simply abide. Most persist in an Advent period of active waiting. They see their journey as a vocation in which they become as big for the world as they are for their children.

The Church of All Creatures Great and Small lives up to its name not because it is perfect. It lives up to its name because it offers its people more than a moment. The congregation knows that God's kingdom is always near and that new life always brings new brokenness and that brokenness takes time. The people believe that God has blessed the worship at All Creatures Church where doors are portals, diversity is welcome, the liturgy incorporates the least of these, and a child leads them. Sometimes they are one. Other times they are many. Always, they worship. In spite of themselves, they have become a small sacrament in God's great kingdom.

Bibliography

Aasgaard, Reidar. "Like a Child: Paul's Rhetorical Uses of Childhood." In *The Child in the Bible*, edited by Marcia J. Bunge, Terence E. Fretheim, and Beverly Roberts Gaventa, 249–77. Grand Rapids: Eerdmans, 2008.

———. *The Childhood of Jesus: Decoding the Apocryphal Infancy Gospel of Thomas.* Eugene, OR: Cascade, 2009.

Anderson, Phillip J. "Mystic Chords of Memory: Some Thought on Music and Communication in the Evangelical Covenant Church, Past and Present." *Covenant Quarterly* 66, no. 4 (November 2007) 19–39.

Anderson, E. Byron. "Liturgical Catechesis: Congregational Practice as Formation." *Religious Education* 92, no. 3 (Summer 1997) 349–62.

Apostolos-Cappadona, Diane, ed. *The Sacred Play of Children.* New York: Seabury, 1983.

Aquinas, Thomas, Saint. *Summa Theologica.* Second and revised edition, 1920. Translated by the Fathers of the English Dominican Province. http://www.newadvent.org/summa/2062.htm.

Augustine of Hippo, Saint. *On the Trinity.* Translated by Arthur West Haddan. From *Nicene and Post-Nicene Fathers, First Series*, vol. 3. Edited by Philip Schaff. Buffalo, NY: Christian Literature Publishing Co., 1887. Revised and edited for New Advent by Keven Knight. http://www.newadvent.org/fathers/1301.htm.

Bakke, O. M. *When Children Became People: The Birth of Childhood in Early Christianity.* Translated by Brian McNeil. Minneapolis: Fortress, 2005.

Bantum, Brian. "New Birth and the Realities of Race: What Happens When Our Understanding of Discipleship Leads Us to a Cultural as Well as Spiritual Conversion?" *Covenant Companion* (September 2012) 10–15.

———. *Redeeming Mulatto: A Theology of Race and Christian Hybridity.* Waco, TX: Baylor University Press, 2010.

Bañuelas, Arturo J., ed. *Mestizo Christianity: Theology from the Latino Perspective.* Eugene, OR: Wipf and Stock, 2004.

Basil of Caesarea, Saint. *De Spiritu Sancto.* Translated by Blomfield Jackson. From *Nicene and Post-Nicene Fathers, Second Series*, vol. 8. Edited by Philip Schaff and Jenry Wace. Buffalo, NY: Christian Literature Publishing Co., 1895. Revised and edited for New Advent by Kevin Knight. http://www.newadvent.org/fathers/3203.htm.

———. *Letters.* Translated by Blomfield Jackson. From *Nicene and Post-Nicene Fathers, Second Series*, vol. 8. Edited by Philip Schaff and Jenry Wace. Buffalo, NY: Christian Literature Publishing Co., 1895. Revised and edited for New Advent by Kevin Knight. http://www.newadvent.org/fathers/3202.htm.

Berry, Wendell. "It Wasn't Me." Short story in *That Distant Land*. Berkeley, CA: Counterpoint, 2004.

Berryman, Jerome. *Children and the Theologians: Clearing the Way for Grace*. New York: Morehouse, 2009.

———. *Godly Play: A Way of Religious Education*. San Francisco: HarperSanFrancisco, 1991.

Beste, Jennifer. "The Status of Children within the Roman Catholic Church." In *Children and Childhood in American Religions*, edited by Don S. Browning and Bonnie J. Miller-McLemore, 71–84. Rutgers Series in Childhood Studies. New Brunswick, NJ: Rutgers University Press, 2009.

———. "Children Speak: Catholic Second Graders' Agency and Experiences in the Sacrament of Reconciliation." *Sociology of Religion* 72, no. 3 (2011) 327–50.

Bonaventure, Saint. *The Soul's Journey into God*. The Classics of Western Spirituality Series. Edited by Ewert Cousins. Mahwah, NJ: Paulist, 1978.

Brink, Emily R. "Who's the Host: We May Be Getting Carried Away with Kierkegaard's Analogy." *Reformed Worship* 9, no. 33 (Fall 1994) 2.

Brown, William. "To Discipline without Destruction: The Multifaceted Profile of the Child in Proverbs." In *The Child in the Bible*, edited by Marcia J. Bunge, Terence E. Fretheim, and Beverly Roberts Gaventa, 63–81. Grand Rapids: Eerdmans, 2008.

Browning, Don S., and Bonnie J. Miller-McLemore. *Children and Childhood in American Religions*. Rutgers Series in Childhood Studies. New Brunswick, NJ: Rutgers University Press, 2009.

Bruckner, James K. "Boundary and Freedom: Blessings in the Garden of Eden." *Covenant Quarterly* 57, no. 1 (1999) 15–35.

———. *Healthy Human Life: A Biblical Witness*. Eugene, OR: Cascade, 2012.

———. "A Primer on God's Created Glory: Toward a Biblical Ecology." Lecture given in Old Testament I, North Park Theological Seminary, Chicago, 2002

Bunge, Marcia J. "The Vocation of the Child: Theological Perspectives on the Particular and Paradoxical Roles and Responsibilities of Children." In *The Vocation of the Child*, Religion, Marriage and Family Series, edited by Don S. Browning and John Witte Jr., 31–52. Grand Rapids: Eerdmans, 2008.

Bunge, Marcia J., ed. *The Child in Christian Thought*. Grand Rapids: Eerdmans, 2001.

Bunge, Marcia J., Terence E. Fretheim, and Beverly Roberts Gaventa, eds. *The Child in the Bible*. Grand Rapids: Eerdmans, 2008.

Burger, Steve. "Christian Formation in the Local Church." Presentation, Formation Leadership Retreat, San Andreas, CA, August 20, 2011.

Burkhardt, John E. *Worship: A Searching Examination of the Liturgical Experience*. Philadelphia: Westminster, 1982.

Bushnell, Horace. *Christian Nurture*. Grand Rapids: Baker, 1979.

Calvin, John. *Calvin's Institutes: A New Compend*. Edited by Hugh T. Kerr. Louisville: Westminster John Knox, 1989.

Carroll, M. Daniel. "Can the Prophets Shed Light on Our Worship Wars? How Amos Evaluates Religious Ritual." *Stone-Campbell Journal* 8, no. 2 (2005) 215–27.

———. "Seeking the Virtues Among the Prophets: The Book of Amos as a Test Case." *Ex Auditu* 17 (2001) 77–96.

Cavalletti, Sofia, ed. *The Good Shepherd and the Child: A Joyful Journey*. Chicago: Liturgy Training Publications, 1996.

Cavalletti, Sofia. *Living Liturgy: Elementary Reflections*. Chicago: Liturgy Training Publications, 1998.

———. *The Religious Potential of the Child 6 to 12 Years Old: A Description of the Experience*. Translated by Rebekah Rojcewicz and Alan R. Perry. Chicago: Liturgy Training Publications, 2002.

———. *The Religious Potential of the Child: The Description of an Experience with Children from Ages Three to Six*. Translated by Patricia M. Coulter and Julie M. Coulter. Ramsey, NJ: Paulist, 1983.

———. *The Religious Potential of the Child: Experiencing Scripture and Liturgy with Young Children*. Translated by Patricia M. Coulter and Julie M. Coulter. Chicago: Liturgy Training Publications, 1983.

Chittister, Joan. *The Rule of St. Benedict: A Spirituality for the Twenty-First Century*. New York: Crossroad, 1992.

Clement of Alexandria. *Christ the Educator: Clement of Alexandria*. Translated by Simon P. Wood. New York: Fathers of the Church, Inc., 1954.

Clifton-Soderstrom, Karl. "Fearful Greed and Trembling Hope: The Timely Vice and Virtue." *Covenant Companion* (January 2010) 18–21.

———. "Love, the Very Name of God." *Covenant Companion* (April 2010) 24–27.

———. "When All Things are Wearisome: Understanding the Sloth of Our Busy Lives." *Covenant Companion* (November 2009) 18–21.

Clifton-Soderstrom, Michelle A. "Beyond the Blessed/Cursed Dichotomy: Barren Matriarchs as Oracles of Hope." *Covenant Quarterly*, vol. 69, no. 1–2 (February–May 2011) 46–64.

Considine, Kevin Patrick. "Is the Future *Mestizo* and *Mulatto*? A Theological-Sociological Investigation into the Racial and Ethnic Future of the Human Person within the U.S." Zygon Center. http://www.zygoncenter.org/studentsymposium/pdfs/papers03/symposium03_Considine.pdf.

The Covenant Book of Worship. Chicago: Covenant Publications, 2003.

The Covenant Hymnal. Chicago: Covenant Publications, 1996.

Crafton, Jeff. "Covenant Theology." Presentation, Midwinter Conference of the Evangelical Covenant Church, Chicago, February 2012.

Cyril of Alexandria, Saint. *Against Nestorius*. Translated by Norman Russell. From *Cyril of Alexandria, The Early Church Fathers*. Edited by Carol Harrison. New York: Routledge, 2000.

———. *On the Unity of Christ*. Translated and with an Introduction by John Anthony McGuckin. Crestwood, NY: St. Vladimir's Seminary Press, 1995.

Davies, J. G. *Worship and Mission*. London: Association Press, 1967.

De La Torre, Miguel A. "Doing Latina/o Ethics from the Margins of Empire: Liberating the Colonized Mind." *Journal of the Society of Christian Ethics* 343, no. 2 (Fall/Winter, 2013) 3–20.

Devries, Dawn. "Toward a Theology of Childhood." *Interpretation* 55, no. 2 (April, 2001) 161–73.

The Dogmatic Constitution of the Church—Lumen Gentium. Promulgated by Pope Paul VI. Vatican City: 1964. http://www.vatican.va/archive/hist_councils/ii_vatican_council/documents/vat-ii_const_19641121_lumen-gentium_en.html.

Elizondo, Virgilio. *The Galilean Journey*, rev. ed. Maryknoll, NY: Orbis, 2000.

———. "Jesus the Galilean Jew in Mestizo Theology." *Theological Studies* 70 (2009) 262–80.

Evdokimov, Paul. *The Art of the Icon: A Theology of Beauty.* Torrance, CA: Oakwood, 1990.

Gaventa, Beverly Roberts. "Finding a Place for Children in the Letters of Paul." In *The Child in the Bible*, edited by Marcia J. Bunge, Terence E. Fretheim, and Beverly Roberts Gaventa, 233–49. Grand Rapids: Eerdmans, 2008.

Geertz, Clifford. *Local Knowledge: Further Essays in Interpretive Anthropology.* New York: Basic Books, 1983.

Gregory Nazianzen, Saint. *Letters.* Translated by Charles Gordon Browne and James Edward Swallow. From *Nicene and Post-Nicene Fathers, Second Series*, vol. 7. Edited by Philip Schaff and Henry Wace. Buffalo, NY: Christian Literature Publishing Co., 1894. Revised and edited for New Advent by Kevin Knight. http://www.newadvent. org/fathers/3103a.htm.

Golden Gelman, Rita. *Queen Esther Saves Her People.* Illustrated by Frane Lessac. New York: Scholastic Press, 1998.

Guardini, Romano. "Retrieving the Tradition: The Playfulness of the Liturgy." *Communio* 21 (Spring 1994) 105–14.

Gundry, Judith M. "Children in the Gospel of Mark, with Special Attention to Jesus' Blessing of the Children (Mark 10:13–16)." In *The Child in the Bible*, edited by Marcia J. Bunge, Terence E. Fretheim, and Beverly Roberts Gaventa, 143–76. Grand Rapids: Eerdmans, 2008.

Gundry-Volf, Judith. "The Least and the Greatest: Children in the New Testament." In *The Child in Christian Thought*, edited by Marcia J. Bunge, 29–60. Grand Rapids: Eerdmans, 2001.

Hall, Amy Laura. *Conceiving Parenthood: American Protestantism and the Spirit of Reproduction.* Grand Rapids: Eerdmans, 2008.

Hauerwas, Stanley, and Samuel Wells, eds. *The Blackwell Companion to Christian Ethics.* Malden, MA: Blackwell, 2004.

Horn, Cornelia B., and John W. Martens. *"Let the Little Children Come to Me": Childhood and Children in Early Christianity.* Washington, DC: The Catholic University of America Press, 2009.

Instruction on Sacred Music—*Tra le Sollecitudini.* Promulgated by Pope Pius X. Vatican City: 1903. http://www.adoremus.org/MotuProprio.html.

Irenaeus of Lyons, Saint. *Against Heresies.* Translated by Alexander Roberts and William Rambaut. From *Ante-Nicene Fathers*, vol. 1. Edited by Alexander Roberts, James Donaldson, and A. Cleveland Coxe. Buffalo, NY: Christian Literature Publishing Co., 1885. Revised and edited for New Advent by Kevin Knight. http://www.newadvent. org/fathers/0103438 .htm.

Jensen, David H. *Graced Vulnerability: A Theology of Childhood.* Cleveland: Pilgrim, 2005.

Jennings, Willie James. "Being Baptized: Race." In *The Blackwell Companion to Christian Ethics*, 2d ed., edited by Stanley Hauerwas and Samuel Wells, 277–89. Oxford: Wiley-Blackwell, 2006.

———. *The Christian Imagination: Theology and the Origins of Race.* New Haven: Yale University Press, 2010.

John of Damascus, Saint. *An Exposition of the Orthodox Faith.* Translated by E.W. Watson and L. Pullan. From *Nicene and Post-Nicene Fathers, Second Series*, vol. 9. Edited by Philip Schaff and Henry Wace. Buffalo, NY: Christian Literature Publishing Co., 1899. Revised and edited for New Advent by Kevin Knight. http://www.newadvent. org/fathers/33041.htm.

Johnson, Luke Timothy. *Scripture and Discernment: Decision Making in the Church.* Nashville: Abingdon, 1996.

Johnson, Todd E., and Dale Savidge. *Performing the Sacred: Theology and Theatre in Dialogue.* Engaging Culture, eds. W. A. Dyrness and R. K. Johnston. Grand Rapids: Baker Academic, 2009.

Kavanagh, Aidan. "Teaching through the Liturgy." *Notre Dame Journal of Education* 5 (1974) 35–47.

Keen, Sam. *Apology for Wonder.* New York: Harper and Row, 1969.

Kierkegaard, Søren. *Purity of Heart Is to Will One Thing.* Translated by Douglas V. Steere. New York: Harper, 1938.

Kress, Robert. "Unity in Diversity and Diversity in Unity: Toward an Ecumenical Perichoresic Kenotic Trinitarian Ontology." *Dialogue and Alliance* 4, no. 3 (1990) 66–70.

Lampe G. W. H., ed. *A Patristic Greek Lexicon.* Oxford: Clarendon, 1961.

Lapsley, Jacqueline E. "'Look! The Children and I Are as Signs and Portents in Israel': Children in Isaiah." In *The Child in the Bible*, edited by Marcia J. Bunge, Terence E. Fretheim, and Beverly Roberts Gaventa, 82–102. Grand Rapids: Eerdmans, 2008.

Laytham, D. Brent, and David D. Bjorlin. "Worship and Ethics: A Selected Bibliography." *Studia Liturgica* 43, no. 1 (2013) 169–88.

Lopez, Barry. "Eden Is a Conversation." Online: http://www.barrylopez.co m/_eden_ is_a_conversation__59075.htm.

Luther, Martin. "On the Councils of the Church." In *Luther's Works,* vol. 41, edited by J. J. Pelikan, H. C. Oswald, and H. T. Lehman, 150–66. Philadelphia: Fortress, 1966.

MacDonald, George. *The Princess and Curdie.* New York: Puffin, 1996.

MacIntosh, Mark. *Mysteries of Faith.* New York: Cowley, 2000.

MacIntyre, Alasdair. *After Virtue: A Study in Moral Theory,* 2d ed. Notre Dame, IN: University of Notre Dame Press, 1984.

Maitland, Sara. *A Big-Enough God: A Feminist's Search for a Joyful Theology.* New York: Riverhead, 1995.

Majerus, Brian D., and Steven J. Sandage. "Differentiation of Self and Christian Spiritual Maturity: Social Science and Theological Integration." *Journal of Psychology and Theology* 38, no. 1 (2010) 41–51.

Manastireanu, Danut. *A Perichoretic Model of the Church: The Trinitarian Ecclesiology of Dumitru Staniloae.* Saarbrücken, Germany: Lap Lambert Academic, 2012.

Marcel, Gabriel. *The Mystery of Being.* Vol. I, *Reflection and Mystery.* Chicago: Gateway, 1960.

Martin, Dale. "Tongues of Angels and Other Status Indicators." *Journal of the American Academy of Religion* 59, no. 3 (September 1991) 547–89.

Marty, Martin. *The Mystery of the Child.* Grand Rapids: Eerdmans, 2007.

Menn, Esther M. "Child Characters in Biblical Narratives: The Young David (1 Samuel 16–17) and the Little Israelite Servant Girl (2 Kings 5:1–19)." In *The Child in the Bible*, edited by Marcia J. Bunge, Terence E. Fretheim, and Beverly Roberts Gaventa, 324–52. Grand Rapids: Eerdmans, 2008.

Mercer, Joyce Ann. *Welcoming Children: A Practical Theology of Childhood.* St. Louis: Chalice, 2005.

Middleton, Richard J., and Brian J. Walsh. *Truth Is Stranger Than It Used to Be: Biblical Faith in a Postmodern World.* Downers Grove, IL: InterVarsity, 1995.

Miller, Patrick D. "That the Children May Know: Children in Deuteronomy." In *The Child in the Bible*, edited by Marcia J. Bunge, Terence E. Fretheim, and Beverly Roberts Gaventa, 45–62. Grand Rapids: Eerdmans, 2008.

Miller-McLemore, Bonnie J. "Children, Chores, and Vocation: A Social and Theological Lacuna." In *The Vocation of the Child*, Religion, Marriage and Family Series, edited by Don S. Browning and John Witte Jr., 295–326. Grand Rapids: Eerdmans, 2008.

———. "Jesus Loves the Little Children? An Exercise in the Use of Scripture." *Journal of Childhood and Religion* 1, no. 7 (October 2010) 1–35.

———. *Let the Children Come: Reimagining Childhood from a Christian Perspective*. San Francisco: Jossey-Bass, 2003.

Moltmann, Jürgen. *The Trinity and the Kingdom: The Doctrine of God.* Translated by Margaret Kohl. San Francisco: Harper & Row, 1981.

Otto, R. E. "The Use and Abuse of *Perichoresis* in Recent Theology." *Scottish Journal of Theology,* 54, no. 3 (2001) 366–84.

Rah, Soong-Chan. *Many Colors: Cultural Intelligence for a Changing Church.* Chicago: Moody, 2010.

———. "Soong-Chan Rah: Freeing the Captive Church." *Faith and Leadership.* September 2011. http://www.faithandleadership.com/qa/soong-chan-rah-freeing-the-captive-church.

Rahner, Karl. "Ideas for a Theology of Childhood." In *Further Theology of the Spiritual Life,* Theological Investigations, vol. 8, 33–50. Translated by David Bourke. New York: Herder and Herder, 1971.

Robinson, Marilynne. *Gilead.* New York: Picador, 2004.

Roisman, Glenn I., and Ashley M. Groh. "Attachment Theory and Research in Developmental Psychology: An Overview and Appreciative Critique." In *Social Development: Relationships in Infancy, Childhood, and Adolescence,* edited by M. K. Underwood and L. H. Rosen, 101–26. New York: The Guildord Press, 2011.

Ryan, G. Thomas. "Introduction." In *The Sacred Play of Children,* edited by Diane Apostolos-Cappadona, ix–xi. New York: Seabury, 1983.

Constitution On the Sacred Liturgy—Sanctum Concilium, Promulgated by Pope Paul VI. Vatican City: 1963. http://www.vatican.va/archive/hist_councils/ii_vatican_council/documents/vat-ii_const_19631204_sacrosanctum-concilium_en.html.

Saliers, Don E. "Liturgy and Ethics: Some New Beginnings." *Journal of Religious Ethics* 7, no. 2 (Fall 1979) 173–89.

Scharen, Christian Batalden. "Lois, Liturgy, and Ethics." *Annual of the Society of Christian Ethics* 20 (January 1, 2000) 275–305.

Schleiermacher, Friedrich. *Christmas Eve Celebration: A Dialogue.* Edited and Translated by Terrence N. Tice. Eugene, OR: Cascade, 2010.

Searle, Mark. "Liturgy and Social Ethics: An Annotated Bibliography." *Studia Liturgica* 21 (1991) 220–35.

Smith, James K. A. *Desiring the Kingdom: Worship, Worldview, and Cultural Formation.* Vol. 1, Cultural Liturgies. Grand Rapids: Baker Academic, 2009.

———. *Imagining the Kingdom: How Worship Works.* Vol. 2, Cultural Liturgies. Grand Rapids: Baker Academic, 2013.

Sobrino, Jon. *Jesus the Liberator: A Historical-Theological Reading of Jesus of Nazareth.* Translated by Paul Burns and Francis McDonagh. Maryknoll, NY: Orbis, 2006.

Tanner, Kathryn. *Christ the Key.* New York: Cambridge University Press, 2010.

The Catechism of the Catholic Church, 2d ed. Online: http://www.scborromeo.org/ccc/ p123a9p3.htm.

The NeverEnding Story. Directed by Wolfgang Petersen. Warner Bros. Films, 1984.

Tolkien, J. R. R. "On Fairy Stories." http://public.callutheran.edu/~brint/Arts/Tolkien.pdf.

Torrance, Thomas F. *Christian Doctrine of God, One Being Three Persons*. Edinburgh: T & T Clark, 1996.

Towner, W. Sibley. "Children and the Image of God." In *The Child in the Bible*, edited by Marcia J. Bunge, Terence E. Fretheim, and Beverly Roberts Gaventa, 307–23. Grand Rapids: Eerdmans, 2008.

Volf, Miroslav. "Being as God Is: Trinity and Generosity." In *God's Life in Trinity*, edited by Miroslav Volf and Michael Welker, 3–12. Minneapolis: Fortress, 2006.

———. *Exclusion and Embrace: A Theological Exploration of Identity, Otherness, and Reconciliation*. Nashville: Abingdon, 1996.

Wainwright, Geoffrey. *Christian Initiation*. London: Lutterworth, 1969.

Webber, Robert. *Ancient-Future Worship: Proclaiming and Enacting God's Narrative*. Grand Rapids: Baker, 2008.

———. *Worship Is a Verb*. Waco, TX: Word, 1985.

Weber, Hans-Ruedi. *Jesus and the Children: Biblical Resources for Study and Preaching*. Geneva: World Council of Churches, 1979.

Weil, Louis. "Children and Worship." In *The Sacred Play of Children*, edited by Diane Apostolos-Cappadona, 55–60. New York: Seabury, 1983.

Wells, Samuel. *Improvisation: The Drama of Christian Ethics*. Grand Rapids: Brazos, 2004.

Wengert, Timothy J. "Luther on Children: Baptism and the Fourth Commandment." *Dialogue* 37 (Summer 1998) 185–90.

White, James F. *Sacraments as God's Self-Giving*. Nashville: Abingdon, 1983.

Willimon, William H. *Calling & Character: Virtues of the Ordained Life*. Nashville: Abingdon, 2000.

———. *Remember Who You Are: Baptism, a Model for Christian Life*. Nashville: The Upper Room, 1980.

———. *The Service of God: How Worship and Ethics are Related*. Nashville: Abingdon, 1983.

Wilson, Stephen B. "Liturgy and Ethics: Something Old, Something New." *Worship* 81, no. 1 (January 2007) 24–45.

Wilson-Kastner, Patricia. *Sacred Drama: A Spirituality of Christian Liturgy*. Minneapolis: Fortress, 1999.